The essential resource for form tutors
in Catholic secondary schools

Just a Minute

A three-year cycle of liturgical assemblies
for every day of the school year

Tony Castle

Kevin
Mayhew

First published in 1997 by
KEVIN MAYHEW LTD
Rattlesden
Bury St Edmunds
Suffolk IP30 0SZ

0 1 2 3 4 5 6 7 8 9

ISBN 1 84003 055 0
Catalogue No 1500140

Front cover illustration by Gabrielle Stoddart
Cover design by Jaquetta Sergeant
Typesetting by Louise Hill
Printed in Great Britain

CONTENTS

Dedicated to my colleagues at St Bernard's,
Westcliff, without whose encouragement
this book would never have appeared.

INTRODUCTION

Background

The word *Miracle*, five centimetres high, filled the front page of the *Daily Mail*. As soon as I saw it, I realised how useful it would be for a morning assembly with my form. The story followed of the dramatic rescue of Tony Bullimore, the round-the-world yachtsman, entombed in an overturned yacht for four days in freezing mountainous seas 1,400 miles south of Australia. Everyone believed him to be dead; and by the laws of nature, he should have been. In the four-page report, under photographs, the words of Tony Bullimore are used: 'a miracle, an absolute miracle', 'my saviours' (Australian Navy), and 'I feel like I'm born again'.

As a form tutor and RE teacher, I immediately recognised the value of keeping this news report. It will be a useful resource and stimulus when I next need to take a form assembly, or morning reflection, on 'Resurrection' or 'Being saved' or 'Christ the Saviour' or even 'Baptism'. It has gone into my folder of useful newspaper cuttings.

As form tutors we have a legal obligation, under the 1988 Education Act, to provide an act of worship, reflection and prayer, every day. (Ofsted inspectors will, when the opportunity is presented to them, take great pains to observe and report whether this is taking place or not.) It must have religious content and this should be predominantly Christian. A *good* assembly or morning reflection (call it what you will) will be relevant to the lives of young people and will involve the students, stimulating them to reflection. It will use, where possible, a range of methods and resources. The DES circular 3/89 puts all this in a legal setting with the following directives:

1 The Assembly should be *inclusive*; i.e. it should be a community activity involving all pupils as valued persons.

2 The Assembly should be *educational*; i.e. it should be related, where possible, to other activities or experiences in the curriculum, and should be professionally planned and evaluated.

3 The Assembly should contribute to the *spiritual development* of all pupils.

4 The Assembly should have a *sense of occasion*; i.e. it should help to develop a respect for the 'sacred' and one another.

Of course, as Christian communities, Catholic and Anglican schools would want and expect to start each day with prayer. However, in reality, not all teachers in our secondary schools are Christians, or feel comfortable leading an act of worship. These may need to keep the legal requirement in mind and will certainly need support from other members of the community. This book began its life against this background, offered as an aid to those form tutors, in my own school, who wanted to fulfil their duty but were at a loss to know how best to do so, especially when they were exhorted to follow and use the Church's year as inspiration and guide.

Almost everyone appreciates the benefit of the Christmas festivities that break into the dismal bleak mid-winter with light, joy and an uplifting of spirits. It is not only a distraction but often too a renewal of family and friendship bonds. For the committed Christian there is the whole liturgical cycle, from Advent to time after Pentecost and finally the feast of Christ the King, to inspire and uplift, if used properly. We should not be just encountering this liturgical year once a week on a Sunday; it should be the scaffolding for the whole of our week. It should inform and direct the whole of our worship and prayer life. This is especially true of the prayer life of a school community, for where else will most of our young people encounter both the beauty and the demands of the Church's year if not at school?

In many Christian secondary schools nowadays we have Muslim young people who, once a year, for a whole month, observe Ramadan by fasting from *all* food and drink from before sunset until after dark. In modern terms, and in other youngsters' eyes, that is as near as you can get to heroism! Are we as Christian educators offering the challenge of Lent to our young people? How will they be aware of our own calendar of festivals if we do not help them to *live* them? This book tries to do that; it offers one way of making best use of our short assembly time with our forms. If such a programme were followed, several times a week, for the five years of a young person's secondary schooling, no student would leave our church schools unaware of the dynamic value of the Christian year.

In most secondary schools the form tutor has little time in the registration period to complete the myriad of morning tasks; besides the taking of the register, there are notices for the form, and perhaps money to collect in or letters to give out. It is easy for the morning reflection to be squeezed out. However, it does not have to be more than two or three minutes in length; as long as there is a genuine stimulus to reflection and a response.

Every school is organised differently. Some, like my own, have one whole school or year group assembly each week, leaving the form tutor to cover the remaining four mornings. In other schools the form tutor may have only one or two morning assemblies to cater for. The material here assumes that there are four mornings to plan for.

This book began life some years ago as an eighteen-page booklet produced at the end of one term for the start of the next. The three booklets per year were well received, and as time passed colleagues suggested additions and improvements. It is now in a form which has proved to be of most value.

How to use this book

Please read before use

First, it has to be said that there are certain difficulties about producing a *static* version of a termly assembly guide for tutors. The Christian year has a mix of fixed points, like 25th December, and movable days and periods, like Easter. Saints' days are also fixed by date, but the Sundays (and therefore the week) of the year are flexible. So you may have to look into the previous or following weeks, or into another year cycle, to find the feast day of a particular saint.

The weekly themes are usually suggested by the Gospel of the previous Sunday. If the theme suggested by the Gospel, for example 'Faith', has already had a good airing, or it does not seem at all appropriate to teenagers, another theme has been chosen from one of the other readings. It is the *Reading of the week* which gives the theme.

If you flick through the book, which of course covers three years, you will see that some themes are repeated, for example 'Love your neighbour'. This is because the liturgy continually returns to the basic themes, like faith and the primary commandment of love. We can all benefit from a regular reminder of these fundamental themes.

The short paragraph that follows the theme is intended to 'unwrap' the theme, to make it more intelligible, expressing it in words and concepts that young people can relate to. The form tutor can do a number of things here: read it, think about and develop it and then give her/his own fuller version; or read it out just as it is; or ask a member of the form to take it away, think about it and produce their own version.

The *Prayer of the week* is inspired by the prayer the priest used on that Sunday and can be used each day of the week, after whatever reading or development of the theme takes place. I have already referred to the use of relevant material, for example a newspaper report; if such comes to hand it may be used here, followed by the *Prayer of the week*.

If there is a Saint's day that week it may be used, if thought appropriate and if time allows, together with the accompanying *Prayer of the day*. At least one *Alternative reading*, on the theme of the week, is provided should it be required, and can be accompanied, again, by the *Prayer of the week* or the *Quotation of the week*. This can be written on the board for quiet reflection, followed by the prayer. Or its meaning could be teased out in a short discussion.

The *Prayers this week* gives a focus for prayer, both public and private. This could also be developed – for example, prayers for economic slaves in Thailand, if the teacher, or a pupil can provide resource material.

The *Assembly idea* is offered for those who have the time and inclination to provide a fuller assembly. They are merely ideas which can be built upon, expanded or act as a springboard for something better.

The keynote throughout is flexibility. The tutor should dip into each 'week' and use what is appropriate to his/her own form, and ignore the rest.

Part One

End of Year A/Beginning of Year B

The Year of Matthew's Gospel (A)
The Year of Mark's Gospel (B)

Twenty-second Week
in Ordinary Time (A)

Theme

What God expects

As we start a new school year, we know what our parents expect of us; we know what our teachers expect of us. Let's reflect for a moment; what does God, who created us and loves us, expect of us in the coming months? He wants us to reach our full potential; make the most of all the gifts and talents he has given to each of us. He also expects us to be kind and caring to one another.

Reading of the week

Romans 12:1-2

Prayer of the week

Almighty Father, as we begin a new year,
  may we use the opportunity to make a new start.
Fill our hearts with love of you,
  increase our faith and give us the determination
  to work to become the people you want us to be.
Amen.

• 3rd September

St Gregory the Great, Pope and Apostle of England
The influence of this famous pope, who lived 1,400 years ago, reaches to our own time; he is called the 'Apostle of England' because he sent Augustine from Rome to convert England. The story is that one day he walked through the slave market and saw some handsome blond slaves for sale. 'Where are these from?' he asked. He was told that they were from the land of the Angles. 'Not Angles but angels,' he replied; and he arranged for Augustine to go to the land of the Angles (England).

Quotation from St Gregory
Patience is the root and guardian of all the virtues

Prayer of the day

Father, you guide your people with kindness
  and govern us with love.
We thank you, today, for the Christian Faith
  that came to England through the insistence
  of St Gregory. Amen.

Alternative readings

1 Peter 1:13-16
Romans 12:9-17

Prayers this week

For all our new pupils and students, especially Year 7.

Assembly idea

Take an alarm clock to the form base; set it for a minute or two after you intend to start the assembly. When it goes off speak of getting out of bed to start a new day; it calls us to action, likewise a new term calls us to action.

Twenty-third Week
in Ordinary Time (A)

Theme

Encouragement

We all need it: young and old, females and males, pupils and teachers; everyone, without exception, needs encouragement. It is not easy being a new pupil in Year 7 nor is it easy to be the headteacher. The most encouraging thought is that we are loved, that people care about us. Everything in the Christian life centres upon love, upon accepting one another; that is the only debt we owe one another.

Reading of the week

Romans 13:8-10

Prayer of the week

God our Father, you have reached out to us in love
    and drawn us into the circle of your life.
May we share with one another
    the encouragement that we draw from you,
      so that we may all experience the warmth of your love.
Amen.

Quotation of the week

Correction does much, but encouragement does more.
Encouragement after censure is as the sun after a shower. (Goethe)

• Also this week

Catholics are encouraged to think about the work of the Catholic Association for Racial Justice.

Alternative readings

Philemon 4-7
Philippians 2:1-4

Prayers this week

For anyone in our school community who feels depressed, anxious or discouraged at present.

Assembly ideas

1 Write the theme 'Encouragement' on the board. Leave a space then underneath write 'Racial Justice'. Ask if anyone can see any connection between the theme of the week and racial justice. (Answer: those of a different race do not need prejudice, they need encouragement.)

2 Before the morning reflection write the word 'Encouragement' on the board. Ask for words or phrases that encourage people, like 'Well done', 'That was great!', etc. When there are sufficient, suggest that each of us today uses some of them to encourage one another.

Twenty-fourth Week
in Ordinary Time (A)

Theme

Forgiving one another

One of the most important ideals that Jesus set before us is forgiveness. How often should we forgive one another? Peter asked Jesus that question and he was told 'times without number' ('seventy-seven times'). So important is forgiveness that God attaches the condition that we will not receive forgiveness from him, unless we freely forgive those who hurt us.

Reading of the week

Matthew 18:21-35

Prayer of the week

Almighty God, there are times when we need to return to you
    and seek your forgiveness;
    may we offer the same love and forgiveness
    to those who hurt us. Amen.

Quotation of the week

Everyone says forgiveness is a lovely idea,
until they have something to forgive. (C. S. Lewis)

• 14th September

The Triumph of the Cross
The symbol of the Cross has become *the* sign of Christianity; the sign of love and forgiveness. From the cross Jesus prayed, 'Father forgive them, they do not know what they are doing.' It is the sign that is marked on each of us at Baptism and the sign we use before and after prayer.

Prayer of the day

God our Father,
    your son, in his love and obedience to you,
    accepted death on a cross.
May that cross be for us a sign
    of love, obedience and forgiveness.
We ask this through Christ our Saviour.
Amen.

Prayers this week

For those who find it difficult to forgive and are embittered.

Assembly idea

The story in this week's Gospel, the parable of the Unforgiving Servant, is easily and enjoyably enacted in the form room; about eight pupils are needed.

Twenty-fifth Week in Ordinary Time (A)

Theme

Generosity

Generous grandmas are everyone's favourites. We praise generosity, especially if we benefit from it. Strangely we do not often praise the most generous of all persons: God, our loving Father, who has given us everything that we have – life itself, the love of family and friends and so many other things. We need to be so thankful and, imitating Jesus, generous with our time and possessions.

Reading of the week

Matthew 20:1-16

Prayer of the week

Father, guide us, as you guide creation
    according to your law of love.
Fill us with your own generous love
    that we may find this love in each other
    as we help and support one another. Amen.

Alternative readings

Matthew 5:40-48
Psalm 103:1-12

• 27th September

St Vincent de Paul
Vincent lived in France just over 300 years ago; there were many cruel and unjust practices then. Vincent was a model of generosity; although a priest he offered to take the place of galley slaves (who rowed big boats) and took the poor into his home. His work continues today through the Sisters of Charity and the S.V.P. Society found in many parishes.

Quotation from St Vincent
We should spend as much time in thanking God
as we do in asking him for benefits.

Prayer of the day

God our Father,
    you gave Vincent the courage and strength
    to work for the poor.
Help us to show the same concern and care
    for anyone in need.
Amen.

Prayers this week

For the homeless who sleep on the streets of our cities.

Assembly idea

Give out small (A6) pieces of lined paper. Maintain an atmosphere of quiet. With no conferring, everyone writes a thought or greeting like 'May today be special and happy', 'You are a special person – believe it', etc. Papers are folded twice. Collect them in and give them out randomly, making sure that they do not return to the same side of the form room. After they have been read, say the *Prayer of the week*.

13

Twenty-sixth Week
in Ordinary Time (A)

Theme

Acting justly

'It's not fair.' How often have you said that? Children especially are very quick to point out any unfairness, real or imaginary. There are many people in our world who have a very hard life; things have often not been fair for them. This is the time of the year when people in churches, communities and schools remember to thank God for all the wonderful things they enjoy, and collect food – as a thank you to God – for the homeless, or the local women's refuge, etc. This is also Harvest Festival time.

Readings of the week

Matthew 21:28-32
Ezekiel 18:25-28

Prayer of the week

Almighty God,
   you are a just and loving Father.
May we always act fairly and show our concern
   by our love and generosity for those
      whose lives have been blighted by injustice.
Amen.

Quotation of the week

The perfection of justice implies charity, because we have a right to be loved. (Austin O'Malley)

Alternative reading

Micah 6:8

• 1st October

St Thérèse of Lisieux
Thérèse was only 24 years old when she died in 1897, after being a Carmelite sister for nine years. She never went anywhere and few people knew her while she lived, but she is today one of the most famous female saints. How? Because she learned how to make everything in her life a prayer, an act of love for God. (She is a lovely person to learn more about.)

Prayer of the day

God our Father, you promised eternal happiness
   to those who live simply and trustfully like little children.
Help us to follow the way of St Therese
   who lived just like that. Amen.

• 4th October

St Francis of Assisi
Francis is remembered today for his love of animals; but in his own time and for most of history he was known as 'the poor man of Assisi'. He gave all his possessions, even his clothes, to the poor. A shining example to us when we think of CAFOD.

Prayers this week

For the work of CAFOD who are on the side of the poor.

Twenty-seventh Week in Ordinary Time (A)

Theme

Do not worry

So many people are filled with anxiety; about their health, their weight, their work, their relationships and so on. There is really no need, St Paul points out in our reading for this week, if only we will trust God. All we have to do is to ask God confidently for what we need; if it is good for us, we will receive all the help we need. Instead of worrying thoughts about ourselves, Paul says, think kind thoughts of others.

Reading of the week

Philippians 4:6-9

Prayer of the week

Almighty and eternal God,
    your love for us surpasses all our hopes and desires.
Help us to place our total confidence in you,
    that anxieties may not cloud our minds
    and we may think only of your love
    and the love we should have for others.
Amen.

Quotation of the week

Worry does not empty tomorrow of its sorrow;
it empties today of its strength. (Corrie Ten Boom)

Alternative reading

Matthew 6:25-34

• 7th October

Our Lady of the Rosary
The month of October has been dedicated to the Holy Rosary for hundreds of years. This feast day has been celebrated since the amazing and unexpected victory of the Christian armies over the Turks at the Battle of Lepanto in 1571.

Prayer of the day

Lord, fill our hearts with your love,
    and as you revealed to us, by an angel,
    the coming of your Son as man,
    so lead us, through his sufferings and death
    to the glory of the resurrection.
Amen.

Prayers this week

For those in our school community who are worrying about a problem or someone they love.

Assembly idea

Write the following on the board and ask if it has a message for us:
    The worried cow would have lived till now
    if she had saved her breath;
    but she feared her hay wouldn't last all day,
    and she mooed herself to death.

Twenty-eighth Week
in Ordinary Time (A)

Theme	*Acceptance*

The opposite of acceptance is rejection; and there is nothing worse than being rejected by family and friends. Jesus came to help his own people, the Jews, and they rejected him. Then they had him executed! Jesus wants *no one* to suffer the rejection that he experienced. We, his friends, are called to accept everyone; even when the most dreadful things happen we should reject no one.

Reading of the week

Matthew 22:1-14

Prayer of the week

Father, the hand of your loving kindness
    powerfully but gently guides all the moments of our day.
Give us the gift of the same loving kindness
    that we may treat everyone with love and respect today and every day.
Amen.

Alternative readings

Isaiah 25:6-10
Philippians 4:12-14, 19-20

• 15th October

St Teresa of Avila
Teresa lived in Spain over 400 years ago, and was a famous Carmelite nun. She was and has remained important because of her exceptional experience of prayer and the books that she wrote about prayer.

Quotation from St Teresa
Do not think of the faults of other people but of what is good in them and faulty in yourself.

Prayer of the day

Father, you inspired St Teresa
    to show us how to live our lives more perfectly.
May we learn from her experience.
Amen.

• 18th October

St Luke, Gospel writer
Luke was not a Jew, like most of the first Christians. He learned about Jesus from the teaching of St Paul and he wrote his Gospel for people like us who are not Jewish. (See Year C, page 100, for more detail.)

Prayer of the day

Father, you chose St Luke
    to reveal the mystery of your love for the poor.
May we too care for the poor and spread your Good News.
Amen.

Prayers this week

For those, especially in our own school, who feel rejected and unloved.

Twenty-ninth Week in Ordinary Time (A)

Mission Sunday

Theme

Citizenship

Street lighting and the drainage system, along with the fire brigade, police and schools, are some of the benefits of what we call 'society'; and everyone lives in society. That means that all Christians are citizens. Because Jesus asked us to care for everyone, that includes caring about good street lighting, good drains and a good police force – and being willing to pay for them through taxes; Christians should always be the most caring and responsible of citizens.

Reading of the week

Matthew 22:15-21

Prayer of the week

Lord, our help and guide in life,
    make your love the foundation of our lives.
May we care about society and our environment
    and always behave and act
    as responsible citizens.
Amen.

Quotation of the week

Whatever makes people good Christians makes them good citizens.
(Daniel Webster)

Alternative reading

Romans 13:1-7

• 21st October

Anniversary of Pope John Paul II
His ministry began today in 1978.

• 25th October

The Forty Martyrs of England and Wales
In the sixteenth and seventeenth centuries many Catholic and Protestant Christians died heroically for their beliefs. It was a tragic time of religious intolerance. As we remember today the Catholics who died about the time of Elizabeth I, let us pray for Christian unity.

Prayer of the day

Father of all Christians,
    today we celebrate the bravery of those
    who risked their lives for their Catholic faith.
May we be strong in faith
    and loving in our relationships
    with all our fellow Christians.
Amen.

Prayers this week

For communities where there is any religious intolerance and persecution of minority groups.

Assembly idea

Dramatise the Gospel reading; it can be acted out by a willing group of five or six pupils: 'Jesus' with two accompanying disciples, and two or three 'trouble-makers' setting the trap for Jesus.

Thirtieth Week
in Ordinary Time (A)

Theme

Love God and neighbour

Life without love is unthinkable. We can do without most things, but not love. This week we are reminded of the two most important of our 'loves'. The *and* is vitally important. It is possible for a Christian to go to church every Sunday and still not be *good* if love of our neighbour has been forgotten or ignored. Jesus asks us to love God in and through our neighbours (who include more than just our friends).

Reading of the week   Matthew 22:34-40

Prayer of the week
Almighty and ever-living God,
   strengthen and deepen our love
   that we may learn to love you
   in all we do for our neighbours,
   family and friends. Amen.

Quotation of the week   No one can be a friend of Jesus Christ who is not a friend to his neighbour. (Robert H. Benson)

Alternative reading   1 John 4:7-12

• 28th October
Saints Simon and Jude, Apostles
Little is known about Simon except that he appears to have belonged to the resistance movement called the Zealots before he met Jesus. Jude, also known as Thaddaeus, was a cousin of Jesus. You will find a letter of his in the Bible.

Prayer of the day
Father, the preaching and teaching
   of your apostles, Simon and Jude,
   led to their heroic deaths;
   may we be courageous in living the Christian life. Amen.

• 1st November
All Saints' Day
Big families like to get together sometimes. The Christian family includes those who have died and are with God (we call this 'heaven'). Today we remember all the good members of our individual families who have died and, we believe, are with God. They are saints and we ask them to speak to God for us.

Prayer of the day
Father, all-powerful and ever-living God,
   today we rejoice in all the holy men and women
   of every time and place.
May their prayers bring us
   the help we need to be faithful to you. Amen.

Prayers this week   For the Refugee Council and all those who work to relieve the distress of the tens of thousands of refugees in the world.

Thirty-first Week in Ordinary Time (A)

Theme

Serving others

People remember surprises! The friends of Jesus never forgot their surprise when, at the height of his fame, as massive crowds were flocking to see him, he said, 'I have come to serve people, not to be served.' Almost his last action was to get up from the dinner table and wash his friends' feet: 'Now you serve one another, like that,' he said. The true friend of Jesus is, then, the person who, without being asked, helps others.

Prayer of the week

God of power and mercy,
only with your help can we be generous and humble
in helping and serving one another.
Help us to imitate the loving service
of your Son, Jesus Christ.
Amen.

• Time of Remembrance

Seen from God's viewpoint there are no dead people. There are only those alive on earth, preparing to be with him, and those who are alive with him in what we call 'heaven'. Our faith reminds us that while 'death' and 'dying' are mysterious experiences, what lies beyond is as real as what we see and experience each day of the week. We pray, in November, for those who did not remember this and did not prepare well enough to go straight into the loving presence of God.

Prayer of Remembrance

Merciful Father,
hear our prayers for all those who died
in two World Wars and many violent conflicts since.
As we renew our faith in your Son,
whom you raised from the dead,
strengthen our hope that all who died
will share in the peace and joy
of everlasting life with you.
Amen.

Quotation of the week

The service that counts is the service that costs. (Howard Hendricks)

Alternative readings

for the week: 1 Thessalonians 2:6-9, 13
for the season: 1 John 3:1-3, John 6:37-40

Prayers this week

For all those who died in the two World Wars and in all the violent conflicts since.

Assembly idea

Bring in the largest piece of ivy you can find and show it to the form; ask if anyone knows why it has been brought in. (Answer: it is an ancient symbol of immortality and was used in the Middle Ages at funerals.) Speak too of the symbolism of the poppy. Pupil concludes with a prayer.

Thirty-second Week in Ordinary Time (A)

Remembrance Sunday

Theme

Be prepared

If you are going out for the evening to be with a friend, you spend time getting ready; if you are going on a Duke of Edinburgh Award expedition, you have to prepare carefully. It is exactly the same with the Christian life; we are preparing *now* to be with the Father one day. The way to prepare is given to us by Jesus: live and act lovingly and humbly, he says; then you 'will be exalted'.

Reading of the week

Matthew 25:1-13

Prayer of the week

Father, God of power and mercy,
  help our everyday efforts to live a good life.
Faith gives us the promise of unending joy and peace
  and makes known the demands of love.
Remove all selfishness from our hearts
  that we may live as you would have us live.
Amen.

Quotation of the week

You grow up the day you have your first real laugh at yourself.
(Ethel Barrymore)

Alternative readings

Wisdom 6:12-16
1 Thessalonians 4:13-14

• 11th November

St Martin of Tours, fourth-century bishop
Martin was a very popular saint in England in the Middle Ages. He started life as a Roman soldier (350s), was dramatically converted to Christianity and became one of the most famous of European bishops (of Tours).

Prayer of the day

Father, by the example of his life
  Martin of Tours offered you worship and praise.
Renew in our hearts the power of your love,
  so that our lives may give you worship and praise.
Amen.

Prayers this week

For the past members of our school community who have died, staff and pupils.

Assembly idea

If the feast of St Martin is going to fall on a day when there will be a form time of reflection (or assembly), a day or two before ask pupils to find out about the one famous story which is told of St Martin. (A simple reward may be offered to elicit a more ready response.) A pupil who has discovered the story tells it. Ask what that story teaches us. Conclude with *Prayer of the day*.

Thirty-third Week
in Ordinary Time (A)

Theme

Using your talents

We have pupils who are excellent musicians; we have good athletes; we have fluent linguists and talented artists. Some are good at making us laugh and cheer us with lovely smiles, while others are reliable and generous in offering help. A community like ours needs everyone; we all have a part to play and talents to use for the good of all. God has given us talents to use, first for the good of others, then ourselves.

Reading of the week

Matthew 25:14-30

Prayer of the week

Almighty Father,
   protect us in the burdens and challenges of life.
Help us to become more aware of your loving plan,
   that we may more willingly share our gift and talents
   to build our community and support one another.
Amen.

Quotation of the week

Alas for those who never sing, but die with all their music in them.
(William Hazlitt)

Alternative readings

Proverbs 31:10-13, 19-20
Luke 19:12-27

• 22nd November

St Cecilia, Patroness of Musicians
A Christian woman, who in third-century Rome converted her husband to her faith and shortly afterwards was imprisoned and executed for the same faith. One of the most famous of the Roman women martyrs, no one today knows how she came to be chosen as the patron of musicians.

Prayer of the day

Lord of mercy,
   be close to those who call upon you.
With St Cecilia to help us,
   hear and answer our prayers.
Amen.

Prayers this week

For everyone in our school community, that we may all use our talents for the benefit of others.

Assembly idea

Without warning, call out to the front five or six pupils (especially those who are not academic) who have a range of skills and talents – for example, a swimmer, a musician, a dancer, etc. Ask the form what these students have in common. Someone may guess, but it is unlikely. (Answer: they all have talents.) Develop the idea that everyone, not just these five, has a talent, which may not yet be known to them.

Thirty-fourth Week in Ordinary Time (A)

National Youth Sunday

Theme	*Christ the King*

The last Sunday of the Church's year (we start a new year next week) is celebrated with a day dedicated to Christ the Universal King. It is to remind us of the Christian belief that the victorious and triumphant risen Christ will come again in glory at the end of the world. On this day we celebrate 'Youth', our hope for our future.

Reading of the week

Matthew 25:31-46

Prayer of the week

Father, all-powerful God of love,
  you raised Jesus from death to life
  and he is now with you, in glory,
  as King of creation.
May all the world rejoice in his peace,
  glory in his justice, and live in his love.
Amen.

Quotation of the week

Where beauty, truth and goodness are advanced, there the kingdom comes. (Donald Coggan)

• National Youth Sunday

Young people are the hope of the future of the People of God, so the year ends with thoughts and prayers for all young people, their youth groups and associations, and all those who work with young people.

Alternative readings

John 18:33-37
Ezekiel 34:11-12, 15-17

Prayers this week

For all Christian young people that they may remain true and faithful in their commitment to Christ.

Assembly idea

Christ the King
Ask how many royal families there are in the world today; how many countries have monarchies. Put ideas on the board. Very few have survived; kings and queens come and go. Christ the King belongs to everyone, everywhere and for ever. He has and will always attract loyalty and love.

National Youth Sunday
Invite pupils who come from parishes where there are lively youth groups and activities to stand up and describe what they do; and how to get the same started in other parishes.

First Week
of Advent (B)

Theme

Stay awake

This is 'Happy New Year' week, because Sunday saw the beginning of a new year in the Christian calendar. Advent – the 'Coming Season' – has begun and all Christians are asked to 'wake up' and 'stay awake' to the real meaning of Christmas. This is the season of preparation, for the Coming of Christ as a babe; as the Good News and as judge at the end of time.

Reading of the week

Mark 13:33-37

Prayer of the week

Father in heaven,
   our hearts desire the warmth of your love.
Increase our longing for Christ our Saviour
   and give us the strength to grow in love
   as we wait for his coming.
Amen.

Quotation of the week

Let us pray so to live that no crisis-hour will find us unprepared.
(C. Albright)

Alternative readings

Romans 13:11-14
1 Thessalonians 5:1-11

• 3rd December

St Francis Xavier, Missionary
Before Billy Graham came on the scene Francis Xavier held the record of preaching to and converting the most people in his life. This took place in India and Japan and the Far East, about 1550. He was also one of the first Jesuit priests and has been admired in the East for over 400 years.

Prayer of the day

God our Father,
   by the preaching of Francis Xavier
   many thousands of people came to know and love you.
Give us such an enthusiasm for our faith
   that many people may learn from us
   of your love in Christ.
Amen.

Prayers this week

For all people who do not know and understand the true meaning of Christmas.

Assembly idea

'Be Alert'. Ask what happens if a pupil is not alert or paying attention in class: they miss work. The same applies to Christmas; if we are not alert we will miss the real meaning and value of Christmas.

Second Week of Advent (B)

Bible Sunday

Theme

Change of heart

John, called 'the Baptiser', was a startling sight; people flocked out from the city to see him. When he got the crowds there he told them that they had to behave better, if they wanted the Messiah to appear among them. A change of heart was necessary or the Christ would not come. Every one of us could make a good preparation for the coming of Christ this Christmas, by improving our behaviour at home, at school and with our friends.

Reading of the week

Mark 1:1-8

Prayer of the week

Father in heaven, your Son's birthday draws near.
May the greed and selfishness,
    which tempt so many people at this time of the year,
    not blind us to the real meaning of his coming.
Amen.

Quotation of the week

Plato located the soul of man in the head, Christ located it in the heart. (St Jerome)

Alternative readings

Isaiah 40:1-5, 9-11
Matthew 3:1-12

• 14th December

St John of the Cross, Doctor of the Church
A great 16th-century Carmelite priest who suffered many difficulties in helping to reform the Spanish Church. Famous for his books on prayer, classics which are still studied and found inspiring today.

Prayer of the day

Father, you gave to St John of the Cross
    the courage to be constantly unselfish.
May we follow his example and learn to put others first,
    and so come finally into your everlasting love.
Amen.

Prayers this week

For the lonely and depressed and all who will spend Christmas on their own.

Assembly idea

Prepare and display a poster with the Chinese proverb, 'It is better to light a candle than to complain about the darkness.' Ask if anyone is afraid of the dark. Follow with a short discussion on the meaning of the proverb; perhaps include mention of Jesus as the 'Light of the World' coming into the darkness of our world.

Third Week of Advent (B)

Theme

Be happy at all times

Human beings come in all different ages, shapes, colours and sizes, but they all share one ambition: everyone wants to be happy. But how to find happiness? And then, how to keep it? When Nelson Mandela visited our country, we experienced a happy man; a sincere man who had suffered that others might be free; a man who had found happiness through working for others. That is the message of this week; if you want happiness, seek it for others, then *you* will find it; and that happiness will remain.

Reading of the week

1 Thessalonians 5:16-24

Prayer of the week

Father, the whole world looks with eagerness
   to the celebration of the birthday of Jesus.
May we, in our lives, know the real meaning of happiness
   and find it in the peace
   that your Son promises to all who follow him.
Amen.

Quotation of the week

Happiness is not a state to arrive at, but a manner of travelling.
(Margaret Lee Runbeck)

Alternative reading

James 5:7-10

Prayers this week

For all children around the world, especially those whose parents are too poor to make Christmas special.

Assembly idea

Write on the board, 'Happiness is a butterfly . . .' Comment that this is the beginning of a quotation from Nathaniel Hawthorne. Ask for sensible suggestions on how it continues. (The *Quotation of the week* may be used as a prompt.) Complete the quotation after discussion: '. . . which, when pursued, is always beyond our grasp, but which, if you will sit down quietly, may alight upon you.'

Second Week
after Christmas (B)

Theme

Seeking wisdom

With the Internet and the high-tech of these times, there is a colossal volume of information and knowledge available to all who seek it. This week is not about seeking information but about seeking wisdom, which is different. Having all the knowledge of the world at your fingertips will not make you wise. Accepting one Word and living by his words will bring fullness in our lives; then we will be wise.

Reading of the week

John 1:1-18

Prayer of the week

Father of our Lord Jesus Christ,
 the simple dignity of the baby of Bethlehem
 reminds us of our own dignity
 as your adopted children.
May we find your love in each other
 and reflect it in our lives.
Amen.

Quotation of the week

Never be ashamed to own you have been in the wrong, 'tis but saying you are wiser today than you were yesterday. (Jonathan Swift)

Alternative reading

Ephesians 1:3-6

• The Epiphany

(When the Feast of Epiphany falls on a Saturday or Monday, it is celebrated on the Sunday. If this occurs the school may like to celebrate the Epiphany on the Monday.) This is the 'Showing Day' because the word 'Epiphany' means 'showing'; the child Jesus is shown to the astrologers from the East. These non-Jews (Gentiles) represent all those who, over the centuries, from all the nations of the earth, would follow Christ.

Prayer of the day

Father of Light,
 today we celebrate how your Son, Jesus,
 the Light of the World,
 was revealed to people of faith.
Make our faith strong,
 that Christ may be revealed to us,
 in our daily life and contacts.
Amen.

Prayers this week

For the millions of young teenage girls who are slaves in Asian countries, like Thailand.

Assembly idea

Acquire (RE department may be able to help) five or six candles of different size, shape and colour, and display them. Ask the form, 'If these were people which one would be the most important?' (The tall one, the red one, etc.?) Listen to replies, then, without comment, light each candle. (Answer: they are all of equal value. Just as one flame lights them all and all give an equal light so the same life and spirit of God lives in each person.)

Second Week
in Ordinary Time (B)

Theme

Vocation

'Here I am, Lord.' The words of Samuel in our reading sum up the attitude of the Christian who is trying to follow Christ. Ready and willing to help others, and so serve God through serving other people; that is the Christian vocation or calling. We each have a unique value and God 'calls' each of us to make the most of ourselves and develop our gifts and talents, so that they can be used to help others.

Reading of the week

1 Samuel 3:3-10

Prayer of the week

Almighty and ever-present Father,
    you see all that we do,
    but your glance is a look of love.
May you see us imitating your Son,
    Jesus Christ, who was not proud
    and full of his own importance,
    but humbly helped everyone as a servant.
Amen.

Quotation of the week

Our vocation is not to become more and more remarkable animals, but to be the companions of God in eternity. (Anthony Bloom)

Alternative reading

John 17:20-24

• 18th-25th January

Week of Prayer for Christian Unity
The followers of Christ are divided. The Christian Family (that is all those who have been baptised in whatever denomination) consists of 1.8 billion people worldwide, split into three parts: Catholics, Orthodox and Protestants. Jesus wanted his family to remain united, and this week we pray that his wish will be fulfilled.

Prayer for Unity Week

Father of all, your Son prayed
    that all his followers would remain united.
Sadly, over the centuries, we have become separated;
    brothers and sisters of the same family,
    but not united.
We pray, this week, that all Christians
    will love and respect one another
    and work hard to become
    one united family once again.
Amen.

Prayers this week

For all the Christians of our local churches, whatever their denomination.

Assembly idea

Invite a Baptist/Methodist/Anglican or other form member to speak about their local church and what they do. The whole form then prays for that faith community and all such local communities.

Third Week
in Ordinary Time (B)

Theme

Follow me

When is a 'Christian' a 'Christian'? Answer: when that person seriously tries to follow and live by the teaching of Jesus. Lots of people use the word 'Christian' to mean 'a good living person'; but such a person may not be following the teaching of Jesus. You have to be tough to be a real Christian, because it is not easy to do what Jesus asks. It requires courage, determination and a real effort to be unselfish. But those who try are helped by God.

Reading of the week

Mark 1:14-20

Prayer of the week

Almighty and ever-present Father,
    your loving eye is always on us,
    and even the tensions and frustrations of life
    cannot destroy your plans for us.
Help us to believe in you and trust you,
    no matter what happens. Amen.

Quotation of the week

To love God is to will what he wills. (Charles de Foucauld)

Alternative readings

Matthew 4:18-22; Luke 5:2-11

• 25th January

The Conversion of St Paul
Saul was the Jewish pharisee who was converted very dramatically on the road to Damascus. He went on to become the greatest of the early missionaries and a vital thinker who helped to shape and direct the development of Christian theology.

Prayer of the day

God our Father,
    the Good News of Jesus
    was spread by Paul, your apostle.
Today we celebrate
    his conversion to the faith;
    may we remain true and faithful
    to the Christian Faith that he preached. Amen.

• 28th January

St Thomas Aquinas, Doctor of the Church
Aquinas was one of the greatest Christian thinkers of all time. His clear thinking and writing served the Church for hundreds of years. He is still admired today.

Prayer of the day

Almighty God and Father
    you made St Thomas Aquinas famous
    for his holiness and learning.
Help us to grow every day in wisdom
    and in our efforts to do good. Amen.

Prayers this week

For all those young people who were baptised as Christians but have given up following Christ.

Fourth Week
in Ordinary Time (B)

Theme

Authority

Teenagers question authority; it is a natural part of growing up to question 'why should I?' The authority of Jesus was questioned, but it was clear to everyone that when he taught, 'he taught with authority' (that is, God was behind what he had to say). Christians have always taught that we ought always to respect (that does not exclude questioning) those in authority, as long as they are not breaking God's laws.

Reading of the week

Mark 1:21-28

Prayer of the week

Father in heaven,
    from the days of Abraham and Moses
    you have gathered and formed a people,
    from whom you have expected love and obedience.
May our love and our willingness to do your will
    grow and develop.
We ask this through Christ, our Lord,
    who gave you complete obedience. Amen.

Quotation of the week

Authority without wisdom is like a heavy axe without an edge, fitter to bruise than polish. (Anne Bradstreet)

Alternative readings

Luke 4:31-37
Matthew 7:22-29
Matthew 28:16-20

• 2nd February

The Presentation of the Lord (traditionally known as 'Candlemas')
(See Year A, page 113, for descriptive paragraph)

Prayer of the day

All-powerful Father,
    Christ your Son was presented
    to you in the Temple.
May we offer ourselves to you each day,
    so that all we do may give you praise. Amen.

• 3rd February

St Blaise
In Catholic tradition St Blaise, a fourth-century bishop, is associated with the blessing of throats (which takes place on this day) because he saved the life of a boy who was choking to death.

Prayer of the day

Lord, hear the prayers
    of your martyr Blaise.
Give us the joy of your peace in our lives
    and one day happiness without end. Amen

Prayers this week

For everyone in our school who has authority, that they may use it wisely for the development of our community.

Fifth Week
in Ordinary Time (B)

Theme	*Serving others*

The symbol of the genuine Christian is the apron. Jesus took the model of the Suffering Servant, foretold by Isaiah, and put himself at the total service of others. At the Last Supper he got up from the table, put an apron around him, and washed his friends' feet; 'Now do what I have done,' he said. The sign of a true follower of Jesus is that she or he is prepared to wait upon others and serve them.

Reading of the week

Mark 1:29-39

Prayer of the week

In faith and love, we ask you, Father,
   to watch over your family.
May we learn to help and serve one another humbly,
   as your Son has shown us.
Through the prayer of the humble Jesus
   may we die to arrogance and pride
   and grow in humility and peace.
Amen.

Quotation of the week

There is no higher religion than human service. (Albert Schweitzer)

Alternative readings

John 13:1-17
Luke 22:24-30

• 11th February

Feast of our Lady of Lourdes
Today the appearances of the Virgin Mary at Lourdes in 1858 to Bernadette Soubirous are celebrated. It is a day for a special remembrance of the sick and disabled who receive much comfort at Lourdes.

Prayer of the day

Father of Mercy,
   we celebrate the feast of Mary,
   the sinless mother of Christ.
We ask you to hear our prayers
   for the sick and disabled
   who turn to her for help and comfort.
Amen.

Prayers this week

For all doctors and nurses and all those who lovingly tend the sick and the handicapped.

Assembly idea

Have an apron hidden from sight, and ask, 'What is the badge of the Christian?' Accept ideas like the cross, the fish. The first Christians used the sign of the fish, and eventually the cross was generally accepted as the Christian symbol; but Jesus himself gave us the badge of the apron (at this point, show the apron or put it on). Have John 13:1-17 read, and use the *Prayer of the week*.

Sixth Week
in Ordinary Time (B)

Theme

Turning to God

We are told that only 10 per cent of the population go to church; but the moment there is a terrible disaster people appear to want God and turn to him. A famous World War II writer said, 'There are no atheists in foxholes.' People want a 'sticky-plaster God' who will say 'there, there' when things hurt. We must be different and turn to God in good times as well as bad; whatever we do should be offered to God.

Reading of the week

Mark 1:40-45

Prayer of the week

God, our Father,
   you have promised to stay close to us at all times.
May we offer all that happens to us to you,
   the good and the bad times.
For to you all glory is due.
Amen.

Quotation of the week

God often visits us, but most of the time we are not at home.
(French proverb)

Alternative reading

1 Corinthians 10:31-11:1

Prayers this week

For those who feel that they are the lepers of modern society; people who have AIDS; may they receive love and support from their families, friends and communities.

Assembly idea

Write the words 'There are no atheists in foxholes' on the board, or display on a card. Discuss what it means; if it's true. Then pray for those who only turn to God when it suits them.

   On another occasion use the words 'sticky-plaster God' in a similar way. Why do people turn to God as a last resort and ignore him when all is going well?

First Week of Lent (B)

Theme

Forty days of Lent

All world religions have times for going without, doing penance. Muslims have the month of Ramadan (nothing to eat or drink during daylight hours); the Jewish people have the 24-hour fast of Yom Kippur. Christians follow the example of Jesus and 'go without' for forty days – the period of time that Jesus is traditionally believed to have been apart from other people in the wilderness, preparing for his teaching.

Reading of the week

Mark 1:12-15

Prayer of the week

Father, your Son resisted the temptations
    of the devil, while fasting for forty days.
May we too resist temptation more strongly
    during the forty days of Lent.
Assist us with your grace and strength.
Amen.

Quotation of the week

Fasting is more effective than charity, for the latter is done with money, but the former can be done only by one's own person. (The Jewish Talmud)

Alternative reading

Matthew 4:1-11

Prayers this week

For all the people in the world who are hungry, not through choice but because they are so poor they cannot help themselves.

• The meaning of Lent

Lent prepares us for Easter, as Advent prepares us for Christmas. Easter is the most important of the Christian festivals. Christians think of themselves as the 'Easter People' and believe that Jesus not only rose from the dead but is still with his followers. So Lent is to be taken seriously because it helps us to celebrate Easter well and to appreciate the real meaning of the death and resurrection of Jesus.

• Ways to make Lent special

1 It is a time for *a change of heart* – a time for a fresh and closer look at ourselves and the way we live our lives. What needs to be done? We *can* change for the better; we must try.

2 It is a time for *concern for others* – a time for caring. Being concerned about others is a powerful weapon in our fight against our selfishness. We *can* do more and be more generous; we must try.

3 It is a time for *prayer that costs* – a time to make a real effort to speak regularly to our best friend, to Christ our Lord. We *can*, in our own private time, make an effort to pray; we must try.

Second Week of Lent (B)

Theme

Service and sacrifice

Losing a child, through death, is one of the worst nightmares for loving parents. To love God so much that you are prepared to give up a son and have him killed is unbelievable to us today; yet that is what Abraham, the first Jew, was prepared to do, to prove his love of God.

Reading of the week

Genesis 22:1-13

Prayer of the week

Father of Light,
    pour the light of your love into our minds and hearts that we may live good lives
    and give you the glory
    for the good things that we achieve.
Amen.

Quotation of the week

Was anything real ever gained without sacrifice of some kind? (André Gide)

Alternative reading

Romans 8:31-34

• 1st March

St David, Patron of Wales
There are many legends about David. Born about 520, David became a monk and studied under the great Paulinus. He is credited with founding twelve monasteries. He became the principal bishop in Wales and moved his community to Menevia, which is the present town of St David's. A popular bishop, his last words to his people were 'Be happy and joyful; and keep your Christian faith'.

Prayer of the day

Lord God, may we listen
    to the last words of St David, patron of Wales,
    and find true happiness and joy
    in keeping faithfully to our Christian faith.
Amen.

• Giving up for Lent

It is well known that Catholics 'give something up' for Lent. If this means giving up a bad habit, that must be good. If it means giving up, for example, eating sweets, that could be good news for your teeth! Unless, of course, 'giving up' makes you bad-tempered and difficult to get on with. Kindness and love must never suffer when we make a sacrifice to fight our selfishness. It might be better to 'take up' something: for example, going to Mass regularly throughout Lent; or saying night prayers better each evening; or making a special effort, every day of Lent, to help at home.

Prayers this week

For people who give up trying to follow the way of Christ; that they may rediscover their Christian faith.

Third Week
of Lent (B)

Gospel: John 2:13-25

Theme

Free will

No one has to be a Christian. No one has to obey God's commandments; God has made us free to obey or not to obey. The commandments, respecting God and our neighbour, are not easy to keep but the effort is well rewarded. Happiness, real freedom and peace of mind come from obeying God. The odd thing is that obedience to God does not take away our freedom, it gives more.

Reading of the week

Exodus 20:1-17

Prayer of the week

Father of all goodness,
   our selfishness stands in the way
   of the generous love that we should show
   to our families and friends.
May we use this time of Lent
   to improve our lives.
Amen.

Quotation of the week

God is omnipotent – but powerless still
to stop my heart from wishing what it will. (Angelus Silesius)

Alternative readings

Matthew 21:12-13
Mark 11:15-17

Prayers this week

For prisoners of conscience; those who have been imprisoned for their religious or political beliefs.

Assembly idea

1 *Review time* Half-way through Lent, how has each of us made Lent special and different so far? Ask the group if they have kept their resolutions for Lent. (If they didn't make any it is not too late.) Have they prayed more? Done anything extra for others, especially people they don't get on with?

2 Wrap up three boxes: one large, one medium and one small. In the large one with attractive wrapping paper put an old worn trainer (or similar object); in the middle size box (wrapped in plain paper) place a sweet; in the small box (no wrapping paper) put a tube or packet of popular sweets. Choose one pupil and ask them to use their free will to choose a gift. Discuss the outcome; what prompted the choice? End with a reflection on making responsible choices. Pray for those who have made the wrong choices in life.

Fourth Week
of Lent (B)

Theme

Trust in Christ

When we get on a bus we trust that the driver knows how to drive, has a licence to drive and knows the way. So Christians trust their leader, Christ. They believe that Jesus really is the Son of God, and so has authority from God, that he knows the way we should live our lives and the way to God.

Reading of the week

John 3:14-21

Prayer of the week

God our Father and Mother,
    you cared so much for us
    that you gave us your Son,
    as the Light of the World.
May we place all our trust in his guidance
    as we seek our way in life.
Amen.

Quotation of the week

He who trusts in himself is lost. He who trusts in God can do all things. (St Alphonsus)

Alternative reading

Ephesians 2:4-10

• 18th March

St Patrick, Apostle of Ireland
It was Patrick, the patron saint of Ireland, who took the Christian faith to Ireland, and established it there by his own courage and holiness of life.

Prayer of the day

God our Father,
    you sent St Patrick as a missionary to Ireland;
    may we too be your missionaries
    showing everyone, by our lives,
    that you are a God of goodness and love.
Amen.

• 19th March

St Joseph, Husband of Mary
Joseph was the husband of Mary and the foster-father of Jesus. He was a village carpenter by trade. He is now the patron of the Catholic Church.

Prayer of the day

Almighty Father,
    you entrusted your Son into the care of St Joseph.
May his prayers help us to be caring
    and worthy of trust.
Amen.

Prayers this week

For all the Christians of Northern Ireland that they may trust in Christ and work patiently together for peace and justice.

Fifth Week
of Lent (B)

Theme

Dying we live

Gardens begin to come to life again. The dead leaves of autumn that have drifted into corners are cleared away; garden furniture is cleaned in the garage, ready to be put out. The daffodils are beginning to show their yellow trumpets. In Europe the cycle of the seasons helps us to understand our faith. As in nature all appears to die in winter, and then with the spring sun comes to life again, so we too must die to our selfishness and respond to the warmth of God's love and show new life.

Reading of the week John 12:20-24

Prayer of the week
Father in heaven,
   the love of your Son led him to accept
   the suffering of the cross.
Change our selfishness into self-giving.
Help us to transform the darkness of this world's pain
   into the life and joy of Easter.
Amen.

Quotation of the week We would worry less about what others think of us if we realised how seldom they do. (Ethel Barrett)

Alternative readings
1 Corinthians 15:35-44
Hebrews 5:7-9

• 25th March
The Annunciation of the Lord
Mary, the young girl of Nazareth, is asked to be the mother of the Christ; she accepts. This event is nine months from Christmas Day and is the origin of Mother's Day, being the day on which Mary conceived by the special power of God.

Prayer of the day
God our Father,
   your Son became man
   and was born of the Virgin Mary.
May we remember and thank God
   for our own mothers
   at this time of the year.
Amen.

Prayers this week For our parents, especially our mothers, who have done, and are doing, so much for us. We pray for their good health and happiness.

Assembly idea Acquire a packet of seeds (beetroot are particularly suitable) but keep secret what the seeds will become. Go round the group placing one seed in each open palm. Ask if anyone can guess what the dried-up, dead-looking seed will become. After telling them, speak of the symbolism of Easter. A live chick comes out of what appears to be a stone; so Christ comes alive out of the dead tomb (hence Easter eggs).

Second Week of Easter (B)

Theme

Coping with doubt

In the famous story of doubting Thomas, he refuses to believe until he can see with his own eyes and touch. 'Seeing is believing', many people say. Jesus calls his bluff . . . then Thomas decides that he doesn't need to touch. One billion, 800 million Christians in the world today believe in the Risen Jesus, without seeing or touching. Jesus had them in mind when he said, 'happy are those who have not seen but believe.' Faith conquers doubt.

Reading of the week   John 20:19-31

Prayer of the week
Heavenly Father and God of mercy,
    we do not look for Jesus among the dead,
    for he is alive.
Increase our faith that we may believe
    without looking for evidence.
May our faith and trust grow every day.
Amen.

Quotation of the week
Doubt comes in at the window when enquiry is denied at the door.
(B. Jowett)

Alternative readings
Acts 4:32-35
James 1:2-8

• 25th March
The Annunciation
Mary, the young girl of Nazareth, is asked to be the mother of the Messiah; she accepts. By God's power this special baby's life begins within her. This event is the origin of both Mother's Day and, eventually, Christmas Day.

Prayer of the day
God our Father,
    your Son became man
    and was born of the Virgin Mary.
May we remember and thank God
    for our own mothers
    at this time of the year.
Amen.

Prayers this week
For all Christians who are coping with doubts about the Resurrection of Jesus, and any who lack self-confidence and belief in themselves.

Assembly idea
The Gospel story can be enacted in the classroom.

Third Week
of Easter (B)

Theme

Peace be with you

The Jewish greeting 'Shalom' (Peace be with you) is full of meaning and a lot better than 'Hi'. When the Risen Jesus appeared to his frightened followers he said 'Shalom'. We have real peace within us when we are not feeling guilty for some wrong we have done; not being nagged by our conscience for harm caused to others. To wish people to be *free*, really free of anxiety or guilt, is a wonderful wish or prayer for them.

Reading of the week

Luke 24:35-48

Prayer for the week

God our Father,
    may we look forward with hope
    to our own resurrection,
    for you have made us your daughters and sons,
    and filled our lives with hope and joy.
Amen.

Quotation of the week

God takes life's pieces, and gives us unbroken peace. (W. D. Gough)

Alternative readings

1 Thessalonians 5:12-15
Colossians 3:12-15

• 16th April

St Bernadette of Lourdes
At the age of 14 (in 1858) the simple peasant girl Marie Bernard (nicknamed Bernadette) was amazed to be chosen to be the recipient of a series of apparitions of the Virgin Mary at the Grotto at Lourdes. She became a saint not on the strength of this, but as a result of the heroism of her later life. She is remembered by the millions of pilgrims, young and old, who go to Lourdes every year.

Prayer of the day

Lord, we see the wonder of your love
    in the saintly life of Bernadette
    and her witness to Christ.
May her example inspire us
    to love Christ faithfully
    in our own lives.
Amen.

Prayers this week

For those in our families who, at present, are anxious or upset about anything.

Assembly idea

Write the word 'Shalom' (Hebrew for 'peace' and used as a greeting in Israel) on the board and explain it. Suggest that we all use it today, when we meet one another.

Fourth Week
of Easter (B)

Week of Prayer
for Vocations

Theme

Pastoral care

At school we have staff who are in charge of pastoral care (these look after the needs of students that are not about learning) but most people do not realise where the idea comes from. The word 'pastor' is Latin for *shepherd* and comes from the phrase, 'Bonus Pastor' and refers to Jesus, the Good Shepherd (see this week's reading). Those who are involved in pastoral care are acting in the name of Jesus, the Good Shepherd.

Reading of the week John 10:11-18

Prayer of the week Almighty and ever-living God,
     please give us the strength and the courage
     that we need to follow Christ. our shepherd.
May we follow faithfully,
     especially when things in life are difficult. Amen.

Quotation of the week The vocation of every man and woman is to serve other people. (Leo Tolstoy)

Alternative readings John 10:1-10
1 John 3:1-2

• 23rd April *St George*
George died for the Christian faith at Lydda, Palestine, about 350. Many fictitious legends, especially about slaying dragons, have attached themselves to his name. He was a popular hero with soldiers who, returning from the Crusades, brought his fame to England. He became patron saint of England in the fourteenth century.

Prayer of the day Lord, hear the prayers of those
     who praise your mighty power.
As St George was ready to follow Christ
     in suffering and death,
     so may he be ready to help us in our weakness. Amen.

Prayers this week For young people to consider serving Christ in a voluntary capacity in Third World countries and in other vocational settings.

Assembly ideas 1 Invite one of the local priests in to speak, briefly, about *vocation:* in the broad sense as well as vocations to the priesthood and religious life.

2 Draw the red cross of St George (also the symbol of the Crusaders and the International Red Cross) on the board, and ask: (a) What the red stands for? (Answer: blood); (b) Which word links all three? (Answer: rescue. St George was believed to have rescued damsels in distress; crusaders went to rescue the holy places; by his blood, on the cross, Christ rescued us.)

Fifth Week
of Easter (B)

Theme

Using God's gifts

Christians believe that everything that we have comes from God: life itself, our qualities, gifts and talents. We need to be always grateful for all that we have received. We need to appreciate that we can best grow and develop – produce fruit – by using our gifts and talents to help other people. Happiness for ourselves is not found except through seeking the happiness of others.

Reading of the week   John 15:1-8

Prayer of the week
God our Father,
 look upon us with love.
Your Son has shown us his love
 and asks us to stay close to him,
 by using our gifts and talents
 for the benefit of others;
 so that we may all come close to you, in love. Amen.

Alternative reading   Matthew 25:14-30 (Parable of the talents)

• 29th April
St Catherine of Siena, Doctor of the Church
A 'modern' liberated woman who lived in the fourteenth century (known through the 400 letters she left) who not only worked among the poor but also worked for the unity of the Church, persuading popes to do the right thing. Patron of Italy.

Quotation from St Catherine
Nothing great was ever done without much enduring.

Prayer of the day
Father, in serving your Church,
 St Catherine was filled
 with the fervour of your love.
By her prayers may we share in her love
 for Christ's Church and all that it stands for. Amen.

• 1st May
St Joseph, Husband of Our Lady; Patron of all workers
Jesus was a manual worker, like his foster-father, Joseph; both knew the hard daily grind of manual work. For this reason the Church has always supported trade unions and campaigned for just and fair working conditions for all workers. St Joseph was declared the patron saint of workers in 1955.

Prayer of the day
God our Father, Creator of the universe,
 you call people to develop their skills and talents
 and use them for the good of others.
Help us to find satisfying work
 and use it to benefit others and ourselves. Amen.

Prayers this week   For the unemployed and for the young workers of Asia who are often exploited to make clothes for our High Street shops.

Sixth Week
of Easter (B)

Theme

Love one another

The theme-song of *Neighbours* can be our song for the week; the words 'everybody should be good neighbours' is straight from the Gospel of Jesus. Only two principles are necessary for a fulfilled life, Jesus said: *love God* and *love one another, as I have loved you*. So simple; yet in practice so difficult, and that is why we need the support of prayer and the sacraments.

Reading of the week

John 15:9-17

Prayer of the week

Ever-living God,
    fill us with the spirit of your truth, love and peace.
Help us to live by the truth
    and enjoy the peace
    that only you can give.
Amen.

Alternative reading

1 John 3:18-24

Quotation of the week

We make our friends; we make our enemies;
but God makes our next-door neighbour. (G. K. Chesterton)

• 6th May

St Dominic Savio
Dominic, who died at the age of 15, is the youngest saint ever to be canonised, in 1954. He was a pupil of the great St John Bosco, and his short life was a model of kindness, generosity and unselfishness.

Prayer of the day

Heavenly Father,
    we thank you for the example of Dominic Savio
    who showed such unselfishness in his short life.
May we too learn to be unselfish, loving and kind.
Amen.

• Thursday

The Ascension of the Lord
(See Comment and Prayer for Year A or C, pages 125 and 83)

Prayers this week

For those in our school who feel unlovable and unloved.

Assembly idea

Record the theme-song from *Neighbours*. Play it and ask what is the connection between it and the Gospel of Jesus. On another occasion concentrate on some of the words – for example, 'with a little understanding'.

Seventh Week of Easter (B)

World Communications Week

Theme

Consecrated in truth

'Is it true?' we ask, when we are told a really unusual story. Fiction we can handle, because we know it's made up, and we can make up stories too. But fact is sometimes hard to handle. The friends of Jesus wanted to know if it was true that he had risen from the dead. That's a truth hard to handle; to accept it changes your life. It means that Jesus really is the Son of God; it means that there really is life after death!

Reading of the week

John 17:11-19

Prayer of the week

Father of Truth and Life,
   consecrate us in the truth
   that we may discover
   the true meaning and purpose of life.
May we know, love and serve you
   through Christ your Son.
Amen.

Quotation of the week

The only way to speak the truth is to speak it lovingly.
(Henry David Thoreau)

Alternative readings

John 8:42-47
1 John 4:11-16

Prayers this week

For those who work in the media industry: on newspapers, radio, TV and film-making.

Assembly idea

Bring in a tabloid newspaper and show how whole pages (more often on the left-hand side) are given to advertising. These cost tens of thousands of pounds; but do they tell us the whole truth about a product? Do advertisers have influence over the content of the newspaper? Is news ever slanted? Encourage a short discussion and follow with a prayer for those in the media.

Prayer for those in the media

Almighty Father
   your Word of Truth lived among us
   and told us of you and your love.
May all those who work in the media
   tell us the truth, promote justice and peace
   and help us to live in harmony with one another.
Amen.

Feast of
the Holy Trinity (B)

Theme

Glory to the Father, the Son and the Holy Spirit

On Sunday, around the world, all Christians celebrated the belief in the divine 'family' of the Godhead; three persons in one unity (Tri-unity) of being. This belief is unique to all Christians. It is impossible to imagine and very difficult to understand, but it is an essential belief for the Christian faith. The *Father*, who created everything, gave us the *Son* (or 'the *Word*') who rescued us and gave us his *Spirit*, the Spirit of faith, hope and love.

Reading of the week

Matthew 28:16-20

Prayer of the week

Father, you sent us your Son
   to bring us the truth,
    and your Spirit to make us holy.
Through them we come to know
   the mystery of your life.
Help us to worship you,
   Father, Son and Holy Spirit.
Amen.

• 27th May

St Augustine, first Archbishop of Canterbury
Augustine was a reluctant missionary, accompanied by 40 other Benedictine monks, who, 1,400 years ago, landed near Ramsgate and set about converting the people of Kent to Christianity. He converted the King of Kent and became the first Archbishop of Canterbury.

• Thursday

The Body and Blood of Christ (The Feast of Corpus Christi)
Just as in our human life we need food and drink, so in our spiritual life we need Christ to nourish and sustain us. He feeds us with himself, with his words, through Scripture; and with the Sacrament of his Body and his Blood. As we eat together the sacred bread and wine, we share with one another, so the community is made strong as we grow personally in strength.

Prayer of the day

Lord Jesus Christ,
   we believe that you live among us
   and we worship your presence
   in the sacrament of your Body and Blood.
May the same Body and Blood give us strength
   to live the Christian life faithfully.
Amen.

Prayers this week

For those who work for Christian unity so that soon all may share the same sacrament at the altar of Christ.

Ninth Week
in Ordinary Time (B)

Theme

Integrity

Scandals by politicians, and even bishops, cause a great stir in the media because we all expect that those 'above' us should act with more integrity. As followers of Christ much is expected of us – we have high standards to live by; any one of us can give scandal. Acting honestly and sincerely – that is, with integrity – is expected of us all, not just politicians or the clergy.

Reading of the week

2 Corinthians 4:6-11

Prayer of the week

Father, your love never fails.
Help us to show your love to others
    by always acting honestly and sincerely
    and giving the example of a good life.
Amen.

Quotation of the week

The measure of a man's real character is what he would do if he knew that he would never be found out. (Thomas Macaulay)

Alternative readings

Proverbs 11:3
Proverbs 10:9

• Friday

The Sacred Heart of Jesus (Gospel: John 19:31-37)
Cards with hearts on are sent on Valentine's Day; we associate the human heart with love. The symbol of the heart of Jesus stands for that amazing love of Jesus that took him to the cross where his heart was pierced.

Prayer of the day

Father, we rejoice in all your gifts of love,
    and especially, today, the wonderful love
    of Jesus, our Lord and Saviour.
Teach us to show that love to all.
Amen.

Prayers this week

For our politicians and government ministers that they may always act sincerely and honestly in the best interests of our country.

Assembly idea

Draw a large red heart on the board and ask if Jesus would have drawn a heart and put initials over and under it when he was a teenager? Why?/Why not? Christians believe he did that more dramatically for us on the cross. Use Friday's *Prayer of the day*.

Tenth Week
in Ordinary Time (B)

Theme

Our Lady, Help of Christians

There was a time when people used to say that Catholics worshipped the Virgin Mary; it was not true, but Catholics did give much honour and attention to the Mother of Jesus. She has been thought of as the second Eve (see the reading) for whereas the first Eve brought sin and death to the human race, Mary gave us Jesus who brought life and victory over death.

Reading of the week

Genesis 3:9-15

Prayer of the week

God of wisdom and love,
   source of all good,
     may we appreciate the goodness and love
     of Mary, the second Eve, and Mother of your Son,
     and ask her to intercede for us in times of need.
Amen.

Quotation of the week

Mary, our tainted nature's solitary boast. (William Wordsworth)

Alternative reading

John 2:1-11

• 9th June

St Columba, Founder of Iona
The most famous of Scottish saints, he is also known as Columcille, or Colm. He lived in the sixth century and founded many monasteries in Ireland and Scotland, the most famous being the Community on the island of Iona. which became a powerful force in the life of the Church.

Prayer of the day

God our Father,
   you gave us St Columba
   whose missionary work resulted in the conversion
   of many in Scotland and Northern England.
May we be fired with the same enthusiasm
   for our faith.
Amen.

Prayers this week

For single parents who are struggling to bring up a family on their own.

Assembly idea

Write the name 'Miriam' on the board. This is the actual name of a famous person: who? Eve was famous because she said 'no' to God; Miriam (or Mary) is famous because she said 'yes'. When and to whom did she say this? Conclude with the *Hail Mary*.

Eleventh Week
in Ordinary Time (B)

Theme

The Church

'Great oaks from little acorns grow'; the vast Church of Christ with membership of 1.8 billion started with twelve Apostles! All kinds of birds can rest in the branches of an oak tree, and the Church takes and gives home to every kind of person; it is the kingdom of God on earth for every person who shows faith and wants to join.

Reading of the week

Mark 4:26-34

Prayer of the week

Almighty God,
    you are our hope and our strength.
Help us to follow Christ
    and to live according to your will.
Amen.

Quotation of the week

The Church is the family of God. It is seen in miniature in each family. (Ferguson)

Alternative readings

Ezekiel 17:22-24
Acts 2:42-47

• 21st June

St Aloysius, Patron of Youth
Aloysius was an 18-year-old Italian who joined the Society of Jesus (Jesuits) and while a student he bravely nursed plague victims, and died. He was proclaimed patron of students and youth in the 1930s.

Prayer of the day

Father of love,
    giver of all good things,
    we thank you for the heroic example
    and generous love of St Aloysius.
May we be filled with the same love
    and give a good example to all.
Amen.

Prayers this week

For those who lead our Church, that they may always remember the needs of young people.

Assembly idea

Draw a simple tree, as big as possible, on the classroom board. At the roots write 'Twelve Apostles'; across the top, in the tree's 'foliage' write '1.8 billion Christians'. Comment that the seed was planted by twelve followers and has grown into a mighty tree.

Twelfth Week
in Ordinary Time (B)

Day of Prayer for Human Rights

Theme

Human rights

Two years after the end of the horrors and the concentration camps of the Second World War the nations of the world put together and signed a Declaration of Human Rights; never again should such horrors be repeated. Sadly they have – in recent years in Bosnia and in Central Africa. Our role is to make human rights known, support organisations that protect them – and pray they may be observed.

Reading of the week 2 Corinthians 5:14-17

Prayer of the week
Father, guide and protector of all your people,
   grant us an unfailing respect for your name,
   and keep us always in your love.
Amen.

Alternative readings
Luke 4:16-21
Isaiah 42:1-4

• 28th June
St Irenaeus, Martyr
One of the first theologians or 'Fathers' of the Church. He was a pupil of Polycarp who had been a friend of St John the Apostle. We learn a lot about the early years of the Christian Church from his many books. He was bishop of Lyons where he was executed for his faith about 200.

Quotation from St Irenaeus
The glory of God is a fully living human person; and true life for a human consists in getting to know God.

Prayer of the day
Almighty Father,
   you called St Irenaeus to stand up for the truth.
May we have the courage to stand up for our faith
   and never be ashamed to be known as Christians.
Amen.

Prayers this week For the United Nations and its work for the defence of Human Rights.

Assembly idea Bring in and read suitable extracts from material published by Amnesty International about their work (RE Department may be able to assist) – for example on the widespread use of torture.

Thirteenth Week
in Ordinary Time (B)

Theme	*Keeping a balance*

At the circus the highwire acrobat is only successful if he has a good sense of balance. In so many areas of our lives we have to keep a balance; we must work hard, but we need to have leisure time too. We must take care of ourselves, but we must also care for others; we want to be free, but we must respect others' freedom too.

Reading of the week

2 Corinthians 8:7-9; 13-15

Prayer for the week

Father in heaven,
    you call us to reject the darkness
    of selfish pleasure-seeking,
    and walk in the light of Christ.
May we maintain a balance in our lives
    between our own needs and the needs of others.
Amen.

Quotation of the week

There is a sufficiency in the world for man's need but not for man's greed. (Gandhi)

Alternative reading

2 Corinthians 9:6-15

• 3rd July

St Thomas, Apostle and friend of Jesus
Doubting Thomas would not believe; he would not believe that Jesus had risen. 'Unless I put my fingers into the hole of the nails I will not believe.' Then he met the Risen Christ and believed. Tradition has it that Thomas took the Gospel to India and founded the Church in Goa.

Prayer of the day

Almighty Father,
    as we honour the Apostle Thomas,
    may we feel the help of his prayers in our lives,
    as we try to follow Christ faithfully.
Amen.

Assembly idea

Ask a volunteer(s) to walk with a book on their head. Comment that this can only be done well if you have a good sense of poise and balance. The same goes for our relationships in the form: it is unbalanced to give all our time and attention to one person. A wide range of friendships should be developed, and that should include Christ our Lord.

Fourteenth Week in Ordinary Time (B)

Theme

Care for the sick

This is the time of the year when groups and pilgrimages go to Lourdes. In recent times the sick have been accompanied by large youth groups; the young people pay their own fare to spend the week working with the sick. Jesus was rejected by the people of his own town and went elsewhere to help the sick. Many young people also find it easier to serve others far from home.

Reading of the week

Mark 6:1-6

Prayer of the week

Father of the sick,
　　your Son devoted himself
　　to the service of others.
May we look for the opportunity
　　to serve those who are in need,
　　and do it in the name of your Son.
Amen.

Alternative readings

James 5:13-16
Mark 8:22-26

• 11th July

St Benedict, Patron of Europe
Benedict wanted to be a hermit but he was so holy that many others wanted to join him. He was forced to set up a community at Monte Cassino (c. 530); there his monks (the Benedictines) lived by his rule. The hundreds of monasteries throughout Europe spread education and farming techniques that civilised Europe.

Quotation from St Benedict
Care must be taken of the sick, so that they may be served in very deed as Christ himself.

Prayer of the day

God our Father,
　　you made St Benedict
　　an outstanding educator and guide
　　to show people how they should live
　　in dignity and peace.
Grant that, like him, we may prefer
　　your love to anything else.
Amen.

Prayers this week

For any local young people who will be going to Lourdes this year to work with the sick, or for the sick in our local hospice and/or hospital.

Assembly idea

Ask if any member of the form has been to Lourdes, or has a brother or sister who has been; encourage them to speak to the form about this. Alternatively, the newsletter from the Across Trust or Hosanna House might provide a short story or illustration of their work for the sick.

Fifteenth Week
in Ordinary Time (B)

Theme

Dependence upon God

Television addicts are only one group of people who have an addiction; many people cannot get through the day without placing a bet, taking a drug, etc. They have lost their freedom, because they are dependent upon something outside themselves. God wants us to be dependent upon him, which is very reasonable since we believe that he made us. Dependence on God brings happiness because he respects our freedom.

Reading of the week

Mark 6:7-13

Prayer of the week

Creator God,
    you made us and we belong to you.
May we not place our trust in things,
    but realise that we depend
    upon you for everything
    and will find happiness in doing your will.
Amen.

Quotation of the week

We expect too much of God, but he always seems ready. (John F. Kennedy)

Alternative reading

Psalm 116:1-7

• 16th July

Our Lady of Mount Carmel
Carmel is a hill not far from Nazareth, Mary's home town, where the prophet Elijah proclaimed faith in God. Hermits lived there at the time of the Crusades, and these later became the Carmelite Order of monks and nuns.

Prayer of the day

Father, may the prayers of the Virgin Mary
    protect us and help us
    to reach a deep union with Christ her Son,
    who lives and reigns for ever and ever.
Amen.

Prayers for this week

For all the people in our own country who find it very hard to provide for their families and will not be able to afford a holiday.

Assembly idea

Ask the form to bring in any spare or used holiday brochures they have at home. Provide scissors to cut up pictures of holiday resorts into strips 5 centimetres wide and 25 centimetres long. Put strips together on the board, using Blutack to make the letters N, E, E, D, Y. Comment that many of us will go off to these lovely sunny places but many others cannot afford to and some will never have a holiday.

Part Two

End of Year B/Beginning of Year C

The Year of Mark's Gospel (B)
The Year of Luke's Gospel (C)

Twenty-second Week in Ordinary Time (B)

Theme

Living by rules

Unpacking a new video recorder or dishwasher, you find a book of directions, or rules you must follow to make the machine work properly. Little babies are *not* born with a book of instructions; but God our Maker has given us rules to live by for a happy life: the Ten Commandments. As we begin a new year, looking forward to a happy year, let us all, staff and students, resolve to follow the rule of Jesus: 'Love one another'.

Reading of the week

Mark 7:1-8

Prayer of the week

Almighty Father,
    as we begin a new year,
    fill our hearts with love of you,
    that we may find happiness
    by following the rule of love
    your Son Jesus Christ gave us to live by.
Amen.

Alternative reading

John 14:15-21

• 3rd September

St Gregory the Great, Pope and Apostle of England
The influence of this famous pope reaches even to our day; he is called the 'apostle of England' because he sent missionaries (in 597), led by Augustine who became the first Archbishop of Canterbury, to convert the Britons. He was also famous for his many books and Church reforms.

Quotation from St Gregory
He is not wise, to me, who is wise in words only, but he who is wise in deeds.

Prayer of the day

Father,
    you guide your people with kindness
    and govern us with love.
We thank you, today, for the Christian faith
    that came to England
    through the insistence of St Gregory.
Amen.

Prayers this week

For all our new pupils and students, especially in Year 7.

Assembly idea

Take into assembly a book of instructions for a new washing machine/video recorder, etc., and start, without warning, to read out part of the instructions. Ask why a book of instructions is necessary. Lead on to how a young child must have rules to live by. For us, as Christians, the most important rule comes from Jesus.

Twenty-third Week in Ordinary Time (B)

Theme

Open our ears and eyes

Schooling should open our ears, eyes and minds to the wonders of God's creation. As we start another year in our education and progress towards maturity, we ask Christ to be with us. We pray that as he opened the ears and eyes of those who came to him, he will help us to open our own senses to every opportunity to learn; and open our hearts to one another in this community.

Reading of the week

Mark 7:31-37

Prayer of the week

God our Father,
    draw us into the circle
    of your life and love,
    that our eyes may be opened
    to the wonders of this life that you give us.
And our hearts to one another.
Amen.

Quotation of the week

Education without religion, as useful as it is, seems rather to make man a more clever devil. (C. S. Lewis)

Alternative readings

Isaiah 35:3-7
James 2:1-5

• 8th September

The Birthday of Our Lady
We do not keep the actual day of Mary's birth because it is unknown to us, but just as we keep Queen Elizabeth's official birthday so we have this day to celebrate the Queen of Heaven. All birthdays are celebrations of life, so today we thank God for the life of Mary, the mother of Jesus.

Prayer of the day

Merciful Father,
    the birth of Jesus
    brought the promise of peace to the world.
    May today's celebration
    of the birthday of Mary, his mother,
    bring us closer to a perfect and lasting peace.
Amen.

Prayers this week

For all the new members, staff and pupils of our school community, that they may settle down happily.

Assembly idea

Acquire a list or programme of adult education courses being offered locally. Read out a few of the more interesting entries. Did they realise that middle-aged and even people in their sixties and seventies pay to attend these courses? Why? Because you are never too old to learn; people have a 'thirst' for learning; there is so much to open the 'eyes' of our mind. You are not educated to get a job, but to develop your potential as a unique person.

Twenty-fourth Week in Ordinary Time (B)

Theme

Who is Christ?

Ours is a Christian community. We believe that Jesus of Nazareth is the Christ (the Messiah) specially sent by God. Jesus speaks with God's authority; when he says to us, 'Love one another', it is God himself who speaks to us. Our community centres its whole life upon that message of Christ. We become more 'Christian' as a community as we try to live the way Jesus would like us to live.

Reading of the week

Mark 8:27-35

Prayer of the week

Almighty God,
    our creator and our guide,
    may we accept Christ,
    who speaks in your name,
    and serve you with all our heart.
Amen.

Quotation of the week

Christ is not valued at all unless he be valued above all. (St Augustine)

Alternative readings

Matthew 16:13-16
Luke 9:18-20

• 14th September

The Triumph of the Cross
The symbol of the cross has become *the* sign of Christianity: the sign of love and forgiveness. From the cross Jesus prayed, 'Father, forgive them, they do not know what they are doing.' It is the sign that is marked on each of us at Baptism, the sign we use before and after prayer.

Prayer of the day

God our Father,
    your Son, in his love and obedience to you,
    accepted death on a cross.
May that cross be for us a sign
    of love, obedience and forgiveness.
We ask this through Christ our Saviour.
Amen.

Prayers this week

For those who cannot accept that Jesus is the Christ, the Son of God.

Assembly idea

Bring in a passport (joke about the photo). Comment that this has details about you, but it will not answer the question, 'Who are you?' There's more to a person than a few statistics. In the same way we only get to know Jesus by talking to him in prayer and doing things for others.

Twenty-fifth Week
in Ordinary Time (B)

Theme

No, to violence

Violence breeds violence; Jesus would never tolerate it. He stopped his apostles arguing; stopped Peter using a sword in his defence; and died a victim of extreme violence. Jesus expects his friends to follow his example. There is no place in a Christian community, like ours, for any form of violence; and that includes people with *attitudes* and violent language.

Reading this week

James 3:16-4:3

Prayer of the week

Father, guide us, as you guide creation
    according to your law of love.
Fill us with your own generous love
    that we may find this love in each other
    and never resort to violent language or actions.
Amen.

Quotation of the week

Violence is always an offence, an insult to the one who perpetrates it and to the one who suffers it. (Pope John Paul II)

Alternative readings

Wisdom 2:12, 17-20
Matthew 26:47-54

• 21st September

St Matthew, Apostle and Gospel writer
Matthew was a hated tax collector who, when called by Jesus, left everything to follow him. (Jesus himself risked being unpopular for his choice.) The Gospel attributed to him arose from his courageous preaching of the Good News.

Prayer of the day

God of mercy,
    you chose an unpopular tax collector, Matthew,
    to share the dignity of the apostles.
By his example and prayers
    help us to follow Christ
    and be faithful to being Christians.
Amen.

Prayers this week

For those who are innocent victims of violence.

Assembly idea

Ask if anyone can tell the group the name of a violent movie or video that they have seen recently. (Accept all titles.) Ask why it is that we don't like anyone to hit or hurt us, but we are happy to watch violence. Can you imagine Jesus sitting down to watch the videos you have just named? If we enjoy watching violence, are we not in danger of approving it and perhaps becoming hardened to it? (This question can be left unanswered.) Say the *Prayer of the week*.

Twenty-sixth Week
in Ordinary Time (B)

Theme

Justice for the poor

'It's not fair,' we very quickly say if we feel that someone has received more than us. The hundreds of millions of poor people in the world must think the same when they learn about all the luxuries that we in the rich nations have. It is not just that we have more than them; it is also the unfair trading conditions the rich nations impose and the huge debt crisis. We should listen carefully to the words of this week's reading.

Reading for the week

James 5:1-6

Prayer of the week

Almighty God,
    you are a just and loving Father.
May we always act fairly and show our concern
    by our love and generosity
    for those whose lives have been blighted
    by poverty and injustice.
Amen.

Quotation of the week

A poor man with nothing in his belly needs hope more than bread.
(George Bernanos)

Alternative readings

Amos 8:4-7
James 2:14-17

• 1st October

St Thérèse of Lisieux
Thérèse was only 24 when she died in 1897, after being a Carmelite sister for nine years. She never went anywhere and few people knew her while she lived, but she is today one of the most famous female saints. How? Because she learned how to make everything in her life a prayer, an act of love for God. (She is a lovely person to learn more about.)

Prayer of the day

God our Father,
    you promised eternal happiness
    to those who live simply and trustfully
    like little children.
Help us to follow the way of St Thérèse
    who lived just like that.
Amen.

• 4th October

St Francis of Assisi
Francis is remembered today for his love of animals; but in his own time and for most of history he was known as 'the poor man of Assisi'. He gave all his possessions, even his clothes, to the poor. A shining example to us when we think of CAFOD.

Prayers this week

For the work of CAFOD who are on the side of the poor.

Twenty-seventh Week in Ordinary Time (B)

Gospel: Mark 10:2-16

Theme

Like little children

Teenagers like to imagine that they are older than they are; middle-aged people are more inclined to think of themselves as younger, while the elderly boast about how old they are! Jesus says, whatever age you are, unless you become like little children you will not enter the kingdom of God. He means that just as children are open and trusting, so should we be; without any pretence and trusting God as a loving Father.

Reading of the week

Mark 10:13-16

Prayer of the week

Almighty and eternal God,
   your love for us
   surpasses all our hopes and desires.
Help us to place our total confidence in you,
   that anxieties may not cloud our minds
   and we may think only of your love
   and the love we should have for others.
Amen.

Quotation of the week

Hold fast to simplicity of heart and innocence. Yes, be as infants who know not wickedness. (Shepherd of Hermas)

Alternative reading

Matthew 18:1-6

• 7th October

Our Lady of the Rosary
The month of October has been dedicated to the Holy Rosary for hundreds of years. This feast day has been celebrated since the amazing and unexpected victory of the Christian armies over the Turks at the Battle of Lepanto in 1571.

Prayer of the day

Lord, fill our hearts with your love,
   and as you revealed to us, by an angel,
   the coming of your Son as man,
   so lead us, through his sufferings and death
   to the glory of the resurrection.
Amen.

Prayers this week

For all sick children in our local hospital and all who care for them.

Assembly idea

Ask the form the day before to bring in photos of any baby or young child they have in their families. Show these around and discuss them briefly. Ask what we mean when we talk about 'the innocence of children'. Share ideas. Read the introduction on this page, and follow with the prayer.

Twenty-eighth Week
in Ordinary Time (B)

Gospel: Mark 10: 17-30

Theme

The Word of God

Which book beats all the records – number of copies sold, the number of languages it has been translated into, etc.? Answer: the Bible. It is the most widely read book in the world, appearing in over 1,500 different languages. The word 'Bible' may spell 'boredom' for you, but for the millions of people who read and use it, the Bible is the word of God; God actually speaking to us in our period of time.

Reading of the week
Hebrews 4:12-13

Prayer of the week
Father, the hand of your loving kindness
    powerfully but gently guides
    all the moments of our day.
Give us the gift of the same loving kindness
    that we may treat everyone with love and respect
    today and every day.
Amen.

Quotation of the week
The existence of the Bible is the greatest blessing which humanity ever experienced. (Immanuel Kant)

Alternative reading
Mark 4:1-20

• 15th October
St Teresa of Avila
Teresa lived in Spain over 400 years ago, and was a famous Carmelite nun. She was and has remained important because of her exceptional experience of prayer and the books she wrote about prayer.

Prayer of the day
Father, you inspired St Teresa
    to show us how to live our lives more perfectly.
May we learn from her experience.
Amen.

Prayers this week
For the work of the Bible Society, the translators, and all those who make the Bible available to the world.

Assembly idea
Ask the form a riddle: 'Which book is a book and a collection of books as well?' (Write it on the board.) The Bible is the answer because it is bound as a book, and used as a single book, but in reality it is a collection or library of books – for example, the Book of Genesis. End with the quotation from Kant and the prayer.

Twenty-ninth Week in Ordinary Time (B)

Theme

Redemptive suffering

Pain is bad news, unless it warns us of some health problem that needs prompt attention. None of us likes to suffer; it is alien to all that we hope for and expect. If by accepting pain and suffering we can put something right for someone else – for example, a mother goes through a painful marrow transplant operation to save her daughter with leukaemia – that's redemptive suffering. Jesus accepted the painful death of the cross to save us from the pain of being cut off from God; he redeemed us.

Reading for the week

Isaiah 53:10-11

Prayer of the week

Lord our God, Father of all,
    your Son made the sacrifice of his life
    to free us from the effects of sin.
May we so love one another
    that we may be prepared to make sacrifices
    to help and support one another. Amen.

Quotation of the week

Man's strongest instinct is to self-preservation; grace's highest call is to self-sacrifice. (Paul Frost)

Alternative readings

Hebrews 4:14-16
Mark 10:35-40

• 18th October

St Luke, Gospel writer
Luke was a Gentile (non-Jewish) doctor, who never knew Jesus; he learned about Jesus from St Paul. He wrote down the teaching of St Paul and emphasised in his Gospel that the Good News is for everyone. He also wrote the Acts of the Apostles.

Prayer of the day

Father, you chose St Luke, the evangelist,
    to reveal by his preaching and writing
    the mystery of your love for the poor.
May we too care for the poor
    and spread the Good News,
    as St Luke did. Amen.

Prayers this week

For all those sick and elderly people in our locality who have to cope every day with pain and discomfort.

Assembly idea

Arrive in the form room with a few paracetamol, aspirin or similar pain-relief tablets in a pocket. Begin by saying, 'I have some drugs in my pocket' – that will get attention! After a short delay, produce them and point out that most modern drugs are used for pain relief. What would it be like to have an operation without anaesthetic? Can you imagine what it would be like to have an iron nail driven through your wrist without any pain relief? That is what happened to Jesus; for love of us.

Theme

An everlasting priesthood

Unlike his cousin John, Jesus was not born into a priestly family so he was not a Jewish priest. However, because he was the Messiah (or Christ) and he was both a man and God, he had a special 'go-between' role to play. He could (and still can) speak for all humans; and, as God, he can tell us what God expects of us. That's what a priest does; so Jesus is our High Priest.

Reading of the week

Hebrews 5:1-6

Prayer of the week

Almighty and ever-living God,
    strengthen our faith, our hope and our love;
    that we may place all our confidence in Christ
    as our High Priest,
    ever-living to make intercession for us.
Amen.

Quotation of the week

People do not *belong* to the Church, nor do they *have a role* in the Church, rather, through Baptism, *they are* the Church. (L. Doohan)

Alternative reading

Hebrews 7:23-27

• 1st November

All Saints' Day (See Year C, page 102)

• 2nd November

All Souls' Day (See Year C, page 102)

Prayers this week

For our priests who serve our neighbouring parishes.

Assembly idea

Dramatise the Gospel story. Then reflect on how in the crowd with Jesus there would have been priests who worked in the temple, businessmen, Sadducees from the local rich families, etc. But not one of those is named, or remembered 2,000 years later; only the man with real faith, the poor blind beggar!

Thirty-first Week
in Ordinary Time (B)

Theme

Love with all your heart

The whole of the teaching of the Bible, and of Jesus, can be summed up and written on the back of a postage stamp: 'Love God, love your neighbour.' Simple to say, but hard to do. 'With all your heart' means loving with a real effort, not coasting along. It means going out of our way to be loving at home (and that is one way of loving God), kind and caring towards people we don't get on with (that's another way of loving God).

Reading of the week   Mark 12:28-34

Prayer of the week

Almighty and ever-living God,
    strengthen our faith, hope and love.
Help us to grow in love
    and show real concern and care
    for all those we live and work with. Amen.

Quotation of the week   Love your neighbour, even when he plays the trombone. (Jewish proverb)

Alternative readings   Use those for All Saints' Day or All Souls' Day on page 102.

• 1st November

All Saints' Day
All those who die in friendship with God are his saints. A tiny few are given the title *Saint*, but most, deceased members of our own families and friends, are in the happiness of God (heaven) and we can ask them to pray for us.

Prayer of the day

Father, all-powerful and ever-living God,
    today we rejoice in the holy men and women
    who are with you in glory.
May their prayers bring us
    your love and forgiveness. Amen.

• 2nd November

All Souls' Day
As Catholics we believe that many of our relatives and friends, when they die, have not lived good enough lives to go straight into heaven; nor bad enough to be punished for ever. So their entry into heaven is delayed, while they are prepared and we pray for them.

Prayer of the Day

Merciful Father, as we renew our faith
    in your Son, whom you raised from the dead,
    strengthen our hope that all those who have died
    may share in his resurrection.
We make this prayer through him
    who lives and reigns for ever. Amen.

Prayers this week   For those who have died; especially past pupils and teachers.

Thirty-second Week
in Ordinary Time (B)

Remembrance Sunday

Theme	*Generosity*

God is never mean; he is always more generous than we deserve. The poor widow in this week's Gospel story realised that and gave everything she had. It is a fact of life that the poor are more likely to be generous than the rich. The rich are inclined to hang on to their money and not share. May we who live comfortably in a rich Western nation not attract the condemnation of Jesus who said, 'Woe to you who are rich.'

Reading of the week
Mark 12:38-44

Prayer of the week
Almighty Father,
   strong is your justice and rich is your mercy.
May we so care about the poor of your family
   that we never miss an opportunity
   to help a person in need.
Amen.

Quotation of the week
If you are not generous with a meagre income, you will never be generous with abundance. (Harold Nye)

Alternative reading
1 Kings 17:10-16

• 11th November
St Martin of Tours, fourth-century bishop
Martin is famous for the incident, while a Roman soldier, when he shared his cloak with a beggar; Martin dreamed later that it was Christ. Converted to Christianity, he left the army and eventually became a famous bishop.

Prayer of the day
Father,
   by the example of his life
   Martin of Tours offered you worship and praise.
Renew in our hearts the power of your love,
   so that our lives may give you worship and praise.
Amen.

Prayers this week
For ourselves that we may always be generous with our time and efforts to help those in need.

Assembly idea
(See Year A, page 20, for an assembly idea for St Martin.)
One group could act out the Gospel story and, if time allows, another group could present a modern equivalent.

Thirty-third Week
in Ordinary Time (B)

Theme

Hope

If you want a career in nursing, engineering, catering, or whatever, you have a goal or a target to aim for; what you hope to achieve in the future decides how you act now. This is *Hope* week for Christians. All Christians hope in the future to meet Christ, either at death or at the end of the world. How Christ's friends act now will decide if the goal or target is achieved. Hope is not enough, it has to inspire action now.

Reading of the week

Mark 13:24-32

Prayer of the week

Father in heaven,
    you promised us salvation and future happiness
    through the final coming of your Son,
    our Lord Jesus Christ.
Help us to make our hope real
    by living as Jesus asked
    and showed us by his care for others.
Amen.

Quotation of the week

What oxygen is to the lungs, such is hope for the meaning of life.
(Emil Brunner)

Alternative readings

Revelation 21:1-7
1 John 3:1-3

• 16th November

St Edmund Rich, Archbishop of Canterbury
A learned and saintly bishop who was best remembered as a teacher; he experienced visions to do with the Holy Trinity (hence his symbol of three suns). He died in 1240.

Prayer of the day

Father of all wisdom and knowledge,
    your holy bishop, Edmund,
    was devoted to teaching
    and helping others to learn about you;
    may we grow daily in our knowledge
    and love of you.
Amen.

Prayer this week

For those in our local community who are lonely and depressed and have no hope for the future.

Assembly idea

Refer to (or, if possible, show) the episode in the film *Dead Poets' Society* when Robin Williams, as the English teacher, takes his students into the college entrance hall and they look at the photos of past students. 'Where are they now?' asks Williams. 'See they are full of health and hope, but they are now old people and some are dead; so seize the day. *Carpe Diem.*' 'Gather ye rosebuds while ye may.'

Thirty-fourth Week in Ordinary Time (B)

National Youth Sunday

Theme	*Christ the King*

The last Sunday of the Church's year (we start a new year next week) is celebrated with a day dedicated to Christ the Universal King. It is to remind us of the Christian belief that the victorious and triumphant risen Christ will come again in glory at the end of the world. On this day we celebrate youth, our hope for our future.

Reading of the week

John 18:33-37

Prayer of the week

Father, all-powerful God of love,
    you raised Jesus from death to life
    and he is now with you, in glory,
    as King of Creation.
May all the world rejoice in his peace,
    glory in his justice, to live in his love.
Amen.

Quotation of the week

The kingdom of God is a kingdom of love; and love is never a stagnant pool. (Henry Du Bose)

• National Youth Sunday

Young people are the hope of the future of the People of God, so the year ends with thoughts and prayers for all young people, their youth groups and associations, and all those who work with young people.

Alternative readings

Matthew 25:31-46
Revelation 1:5-8
Daniel 7:13-14

Prayers this week

For all Christian young people, that they may remain true and faithful to their commitment to Christ.

Assembly idea

If video facilities are available, show the short extract of *Dead Poets' Society* when Robin Williams (as Mr Keating) takes his class to the entrance hall and asks them to view the future and call him 'Captain, my captain'. Could we call Jesus by that title? Or would 'Christ our President' be more suitable? Why do we prefer 'King'? What does it convey in modern times?

First Week in Advent (C)

Theme

Freedom from fear

To be free. That's what we all want. To be loved. That too! These are the two greatest human values. Doing what *I* want all the time, getting my own way, however, is not real freedom; just as real love is not self-centred. Only Christ can give real freedom, by following his words – 'Love one another' – and his example of unselfish caring. Advent is the season when we examine the question: how 'free' and 'loving' are we?

Reading of the week

Luke 21:25-28

Prayer of the week

Father in heaven,
  our hearts desire the warmth of your love.
Increase our longing for Christ our Saviour,
  and give us the strength to grow in love
  as we wait for his coming.
Amen.

Quotation of the week

One hallmark of freedom is the sound of laughter. (Harry Ashmore)

Alternative readings

1 Thessalonians 3:12-4:2
Mark 13:33-37

• 30th November

St Andrew, Apostle and Patron of Scotland
Andrew was the brother of Simon Peter, and a fisherman. He was called to follow Jesus and chosen to be an Apostle. He is believed to have died a martyr's death at Patras, in Achaia.

Prayer of the day

Lord, in your loving kindness
  hear our prayers.
You called Andrew to preach the Gospel
  and witness to its truth.
May he always be our friend, in your presence,
  praying that our faith and love for you may grow.
Amen.

Prayers this week

For the people who do not know and understand the true meaning of Christmas.

Assembly idea

Acquire a genuine Advent calendar (not one with a picture of Mickey Mouse or Father Christmas on the front, but a Nativity scene), or ask a creative member of the form to make one. Post it up in the form room and arrange a fair system for a different pupil to open a 'window' each day of Advent. (CAFOD have a good Advent calendar each year related to the needs of the developing nations.)

Second Week of Advent (C)

Bible Sunday

Theme

Prepare the way

It is easier to prepare things than to prepare people; it is easier to buy a Christmas card than to make one yourself. It is easier to spend money on gifts than to change your behaviour. The modern secular Christmas is more about 'things' than people. Christians are asked to prepare themselves for the birthday of Christ by self-denial (saying 'no' to selfishness). The gift that Christians prepare to give Christ on his birthday is the gift of their love and trust. Advent is the season of personal preparation.

Reading of the week

Luke 3:1-6

Prayer of the week

Father, in heaven,
   your Son's birthday draws near.
May the greed and selfishness,
   which tempt so many people at this time of the year,
   not blind us to the real meaning of his coming.
Amen.

Quotation of the week

Sleep with clean hands, either kept clean all day by integrity or washed clean at night by repentance. (John Donne)

Alternative readings

Philippians 1:3-6, 8-11
Mark 1:1-8

• 8th December

The Immaculate Conception of the Blessed Virgin Mary
This day celebrates the 'specialness' of Mary, from the moment of her conception (this is not the same as the Virgin Birth). She was chosen, even before her own birth, for the wonderful privilege of being the mother of Jesus, the Son of God. It is summed up in the words 'Hail Mary, full of grace'.

Prayer of the day

Father, you prepared the Virgin Mary,
   even from the first moment of her conception,
   to be the worthy mother of your Son.
Help us, by her prayers,
   to live in your presence without sin.
Amen.

Prayers this week

For those who have no families and will spend this Christmas on their own.

Assembly idea

Ask for a list of things that have to be prepared for Christmas and write these on the board. Then ask how people prepare. How will *you* prepare to receive Christ into your hearts this Christmas?

Third Week of Advent (C)

Theme

Sharing what we have

People are generous to others at Christmas; it is the time for sharing, because *God so loved us that he gave us his only Son*. We need to remember that God gave his gift to everyone, not just his friends. We should not give just to receive something in return; that is not generosity but simple exchange or trading. Christ's friends should give – if only something as simple as a smile – as a loving gesture in his name, to those who may not be friends. This is a time for reconciliation.

Reading of the week

Luke 3:10-18

Prayer of the week

Father, the whole world looks with eagerness
   to the celebration of the birthday of Jesus.
May we, in our lives,
   know the real meaning of happiness
   and find it in the peace that your Son promises
   to all who follow him.
Amen.

Quotation of the week

Give what you have; to someone it may be better than you dare to think. (Henry Wadsworth Longfellow)

Alternative readings

Philippians 4:4-7
Zephaniah 3:14-18

• 14th September

St John of the Cross, Doctor of the Church
A Carmelite priest who, in sixteenth-century Spain, set out to reform the Carmelite Order. He suffered much opposition but became a great expert on prayer. He is famous for his many writings and inspiring poetry.

Prayer of the day

Father, you gave St John of the Cross
   a great spirit of self-discipline
   and an immense love of you.
May we follow his example
   and be helped by his prayers.
Amen.

Prayers this week

For all children around the world, especially those whose parents are too poor to make Christmas special.

Assembly idea

Ask (with appropriate props), 'Why is it easier for me to offer you a sweet from a tube of sweets than to open a box of "Quality Street" in front of you?' Because with a tube of sweets everyone gets exactly the same; with a box of chocolates people start to state their preferences, and pick and choose. So God gives generously to us; we are unable to pick and choose. Let's be grateful for all that he shares with us.

Second Week
after Christmas (C)

Theme

Mary, Mother of the Church

Without Miriam of Nazareth (or Mary, the mother of Jesus) there would have been no Christmas. By any standards she was a unique woman and mother. Chosen by God to be the mother of the Messiah, she carried within her, for nine months, the Son of God. She brought him up, educated him and prepared him for life. Traditionally this week's reading on the subject of wisdom has been applied to her.

Reading of the week

Sirach 24:1-4, 12-16

Prayer of the week

Father of our Lord Jesus Christ,
    the simple dignity of the baby of Bethlehem
    reminds us of our own dignity
    as your adopted children.
May we find your love in each other
    and reflect it in our lives.
Amen.

Quotation of the week

Our tainted nature's solitary boast. (William Wordsworth)

Alternative reading

Ephesians 1:3-6

• The Epiphany

(When the Feast of Epiphany falls on a Saturday or Monday, it is celebrated on the Sunday. If this occurs the school may like to celebrate the Epiphany on the Monday.) This is the 'Showing Day' because the word 'Epiphany' means 'showing'; the child Jesus is shown to the astrologers from the East. These non-Jews (Gentiles) represent all those who, over the centuries, from all the nations of the earth, would follow Christ.

Prayer of the day

Father of Light,
    today we celebrate how your Son, Jesus,
    the Light of the World,
    was revealed to people of faith.
Make our faith strong, that Christ
    may be revealed to us,
    in our daily life and contacts.
Amen.

Prayers this week

For the millions of young teenage girls who are slaves in Asian countries, like Thailand.

Assembly idea

Acquire (RE department may be able to help) five or six candles of different size, shape and colour, and display them. Ask the form, 'If these were people which one would be the most important?' (The tall one, the red one, etc.?) Listen to replies, then, without comment, light each candle. (Answer: they are all of equal value. Just as one flame lights them all and all give an equal light so the same life and spirit of God lives in each person.)

Second Week
in Ordinary Time (C)

Theme	*Unity*

In a community like ours there are so many different jobs to be done, from cleaning the classrooms and preparing meals to typing letters or taking lessons. There are many different tasks but, in a Christian community, they should all be done for the same reason, to build up the community in love. We all need one another. The Spirit of God is present, as the Spirit of unity, to give help and support as we seek that unity.

Reading of the week

1 Corinthians 12:4-11

Prayer of the week

Almighty and ever-present Father,
    you see all that we do,
    but your glance is a look of love.
May you see us imitating your Son, Jesus Christ,
    who was not proud
    and full of his own importance,
    but humbly helped everyone as a servant.
Amen.

Quotation of the week

The responsibility of tolerance lies with those who have the wider vision. (George Eliot)

Alternative readings

John 17:20-24

• 18th-25th January

Week of Prayer for Christian Unity
The followers of Christ are divided. The Christian Family (that is all those who have been baptised in whatever denomination) consists of 1.8 billion people worldwide, split into three parts: Catholics, Orthodox and Protestants. Jesus wanted his family to remain united, and this week we pray that his wish will be fulfilled.

Prayer for Unity Week

Father of all, your Son prayed
    that all his followers would remain united.
Sadly, over the centuries, we have become separated;
    brothers and sisters of the same family,
    but not united.
We pray, this week, that all Christians
    will love and respect one another
    and work hard to become
    one united family once again.
Amen.

Prayers this week

For all the Christians of our local churches, whatever their denomination.

Assembly idea

Invite a Baptist/Methodist/Anglican or other form member to speak about their local church and what they do. The whole form then prays for that faith community and all such local communities.

Third Week
in Ordinary Time (C)

Theme

Christ's body – the Church

We all need to belong – to a family, to a group of friends, or to a club. Christ's followers form a family group, with God as 'our Father'; that family is called 'the Church'. The Apostle Paul described this family group as being like a body; just as there are many parts to a body, with different tasks, so too there are in the Church. Christ Jesus is the head of the body and each of us has a part to play.

Reading of the week

1 Corinthians 12:12-30

Prayer of the week

Almighty and ever-present Father,
   your loving eye is always on us,
   and even the tensions and frustrations of life
   cannot destroy your plans for us.
Help us to believe in you and trust you,
   no matter what happens. Amen.

Quotation of the week

He cannot have God for his father who refuses to have the Church for his mother. (St Augustine)

Alternative reading

Matthew 4:18-22

• 25th January

The Conversion of St Paul
Saul was the Jewish Pharisee who was converted very dramatically on the road to Damascus. He went on to become the greatest of the early missionaries and a vital thinker who helped to shape and direct the development of Christian theology.

Prayer of the day

God our Father,
   the Good News of Jesus
   was spread by Paul, your apostle.
Today we celebrate his conversion to the faith;
   may we remain true and faithful
   to the Christian faith that he preached. Amen.

• 28th January

St Thomas Aquinas, Doctor of the Church
Aquinas was one of the greatest Christian thinkers of all time. His clear thinking and writing served the Church for hundreds of years. He is still admired today.

Prayer of the day

Almighty God and Father,
   you made St Thomas Aquinas famous
   for his holiness and learning.
Help us to grow every day in wisdom
   and in our efforts to do good. Amen.

Prayers this week

For all those young people who were baptised as Christians but have given up following Christ.

Fourth Week
in Ordinary Time (C)

Theme

The manhood of Christ

The Greeks and the Romans had loads of gods, for every possible job; but they were unreal and of no help to ordinary people. Our God, on the other hand, felt so strongly about knowing and understanding our life, that he became a human, just like us. As Jesus, the Christ, he experienced all the daily ups and downs of life, the happiness and the pain. We could have no better friend who knows, understands and can help.

Reading of the week Luke 4:21-30

Prayer of the week
Father in heaven,
    from the days of Abraham and Moses
    you have gathered and formed a people,
    from whom you have expected love and obedience.
May our love and our willingness to do your will
    grow and develop.
We ask this through Christ, our Lord,
    who gave you complete obedience.
Amen.

Quotation of the week He became what we are that he might make us what he is. (St Athanasius)

Alternative readings
Luke 2:21-40
Matthew 7:24-29
Matthew 28:16-20

• 2nd February *The Presentation of the Lord (traditionally known as 'Candlemas')*
(See Year A, page 113, for descriptive paragraph)

Prayer of the day
All-powerful Father,
    Christ your Son was presented to you in the Temple.
May we offer ourselves to you each day,
    so that all we do may give you praise. Amen.

• 3rd February *St Blaise*
In Catholic tradition St Blaise, a bishop of the fourth century, is associated with the blessing of throats (which takes place on this day) because he saved the life of a boy who was choking to death.

Prayer of the day
Lord, hear the prayers
    of your martyr Blaise.
Give us the joy of your peace in our lives
    and one day happiness without end.
Amen.

Prayers this week For local elderly people who find it difficult to get out in the winter months and are frightened to come out after dark.

Fifth Week
in Ordinary Time (C)

Theme

Following Christ

There are 1.8 billion followers of Christ in the world today; half of that number are Catholics. Not all, of course, are good followers, but at some point they have made a decision to try and follow the teaching of Jesus. That is all any of us can do: try and live up to the high ideals and standards that Christ has set his followers.

Reading of the week

Luke 5:1-11

Prayer of the week

In faith and love, we ask you, Father,
    to watch over your family.
May we learn to help and serve one another humbly,
    as your Son has shown us.
Through the prayer of the humble Jesus
    may we die to arrogance and pride
    and grow in humility and peace.
Amen.

Quotation of the week

People only think a thing's worth believing in if it's hard to believe.
(Armiger Barclay)

Alternative reading

Isaiah 6:1-8

• 11th February

Feast of Our Lady of Lourdes
Today the appearances of the Virgin Mary at Lourdes in 1858, to Bernadette Soubirous, are celebrated. It is a day for a special remembrance of the sick and disabled who receive much comfort at Lourdes.

Prayer of the day

Father of mercy,
    we celebrate the feast of Mary,
    the sinless mother of Christ.
We ask you to hear our prayers for the sick and disabled
    who turn to her for help and comfort.
Amen.

Prayers this week

For all doctors and nurses, and all those who lovingly tend the sick and the handicapped.

Assembly idea

Have an apron hidden from sight, and ask, 'What is the badge of the Christian?' Accept ideas like the cross, the fish. The first Christians used the sign of the fish, and eventually the cross was generally accepted as the Christian symbol; but Jesus himself gave us the badge of the apron (at this point, show the apron or put it on). Have John 13:1-17 read, and use the *Prayer of the week*.

Sixth Week
in Ordinary Time (C)

Theme

The Beatitudes

When you come to exam time short summaries of what you have learned can be very useful. The Beatitudes are rather like that; they are a short summary of all Christ's teaching. The list looks simple at first, then confusing because it appears to contradict what we normally believe. 'Blessed are the poor' does not mean what it first appears to. Jesus' teaching challenges us to think; it turns our normal values upside down.

Reading of the week

Luke 6:17, 20-26

Prayer of the week

Father in heaven,
    the loving plan of your wisdom
    took flesh in Jesus Christ,
    and changed humankind's history
    by his command of perfect love.
May we be inspired by the same wisdom
    to seek and do your will.
Amen.

Quotation of the week

The Beatitudes are a call to us to see ourselves in a way that probably does not come easily to us. (Simon Tugwell)

Alternative readings

Matthew 5:1-12
Jeremiah 17:5-8

Prayers this week

For those who struggle with depression and mental illness, that they may experience the love and support of friends.

Assembly idea

Choose a volunteer and tell them they have won £5 million on the National Lottery, but one condition has been attached. They must spend all the money on other people. Who will you spend it on? Will spending it on others bring you any happiness?' Discuss ideas, and close with the *Prayer of the week*.

First Week of Lent (C)

Theme

Worship God alone

The way some people cherish their cars, you would think that they worship them. The way some TV or film stars are treated by their fans, you could say that they idolise them. All Jews, Muslims and Christians agree that only God may be worshipped; we may not make idols of anyone or anything. Jesus made this quite clear when he said, 'Only two things are necessary. Love God with all your heart and your neighbour as yourself.'

Reading of the week

Luke 4:1-13

Prayer of the week

Father, your Son resisted the temptations of the devil,
    while fasting for forty days.
May we too resist temptation more strongly during the forty days of Lent.
Assist us with your grace and strength.
Amen.

Quotation of the week

It is only when people begin to worship that they begin to grow.
(Calvin Coolidge)

Alternative readings

Matthew 4:1-11
Deuteronomy 8:1-6

Prayers this week

For all the people in the world who are hungry, not through choice but because they are so poor they cannot help themselves.

• The meaning of Lent

Lent prepares us for Easter, as Advent prepares us for Christmas. Easter is the most important of the Christian festivals. Christians think of themselves as the 'Easter People' and believe that Jesus not only rose from the dead but is still with his followers. So Lent is to be taken seriously because it helps us to celebrate Easter well and to appreciate the real meaning of the death and resurrection of Jesus.

• Ways to make Lent special

1 It is a time for a *change of heart* – a time for a fresh and closer look at ourselves and the way we live our lives. What needs to be done? We *can* change for the better; we must try.

2 It is a time for *concern for others* – a time for caring. Being concerned about others is a powerful weapon in our fight against our selfishness. We *can* do more and be more generous; we must try.

3 It is a time for *prayer that costs* – a time to make a real effort to speak regularly to our best friend, to Christ our Lord. We *can*, in our own private time, make an effort to pray; we must try.

Second Week of Lent (C)

Theme

Finding out God's will

People go to fortune-tellers to try and find out what lies in the future and how they should live their lives. Christians believe that the future is best left in the hands of God. How do I know what God wants me to do? By trying to find out what God wants me to do with my life; by prayer and seeking guidance from wise and experienced people; by being 'open' to what comes along and responding in a generous way.

Reading of the week Genesis 15:5-12, 17-18

Prayer of the week

Father of Light,
    pour the light of your love into our minds and hearts
    that we may live good lives
    and give you the glory
    for the good things that we achieve.
Amen.

Quotation of the week

If God sends us on stony paths, he provides strong shoes.
(Corrie Ten Boom)

Alternative readings

Psalm 25:4-10
1 John 4:7-10

• 17th March

St Patrick, Patron of Ireland
Patrick spent his early years in Ireland as a slave; in early manhood he escaped to France. He became a monk and a bishop and returned to Ireland as a missionary when he was 60 years old. With great courage he took on the pagan Druids and converted the king. His writings witness to the daily dangers of his life. He died at the age of 90 in 461.

Prayer of the day

God our Father,
    you sent St Patrick as a missionary to Ireland.
May we too be your missionaries,
    showing everyone, by our lives,
    that you are a God of goodness and love.
Amen.

• Giving up for Lent

It is well known that Catholics 'give something up' for Lent. If this means giving up a bad habit, that must be good. If it means giving up, for example, eating sweets, that could be good news for your teeth! Unless, of course, 'giving up' makes you bad-tempered and difficult to get on with. Kindness and love must never suffer when we make a sacrifice to fight our selfishness. It might be better to 'take up' something: for example, going to Mass regularly throughout Lent; or saying night prayers better each evening; or making a special effort, every day of Lent, to help at home.

Prayers this week

For all the Christians of Northern Ireland, that they may trust and follow Christ, and live and work happily together.

Third Week
of Lent (C)

Theme

Repent

One of the most difficult words to say is 'sorry', often because we don't really want to face the truth about ourselves. How often have you heard people say, 'It's not my fault' (when it obviously is!). One of the sure signs of maturity is accepting responsibility for our actions. Accepting that we make mistakes; that we do wrong. Before we can genuinely say 'sorry' and mean it, we must repent. We must feel sorry.

Reading of the week

Luke 13:1-9

Prayer of the week

Father of all goodness,
    our selfishness stands in the way
    of the generous love that we should show
    to our families and friends.
May we use this time of Lent
    to improve our lives.
Amen.

Quotation of the week

It is never too late to repent. (English proverb)

Alternative reading

Psalm 51:1-13

Prayers this week

For everyone who has done wrong and been imprisoned. May they repent and be reformed; on release may they be accepted back into society and make a fresh start.

Assembly idea

1 *Review time* Half-way through Lent, how have each of us made Lent special and different so far? Ask the group if they have kept their resolutions for Lent. (If they didn't make any it is not too late.) Have they prayed more? Done anything extra for others, especially people they don't get on with?

2 Wrap up three boxes: one large, one medium and one small. In the large one with attractive wrapping paper put an old worn trainer (or similar object); in the middle size box (wrapped in plain paper) place a sweet; in the small box (no wrapping paper) put a tube or packet of popular sweets. Choose one pupil and ask them to use their free will to choose a gift. Discuss the outcome; what prompted the choice? End with a reflection on making responsible choices. Pray for those who made the wrong choices in life.

Fourth Week
of Lent (C)

Theme

Reconciliation

We all know about 'making up'. How many times a day do pupils fall out with one another and then have to make up again? (That's what reconciliation is.) This is the season for 'making up', especially with God if we have turned away from him. (We call that 'sinning'.) We can do this at the beginning of each Mass, and through the services of Reconciliation that take place in Lent.

Reading of the week

Luke 15:1-3, 11-32

Prayer of the week

God our Father and Mother,
    you cared so much for us
    that you gave us your Son,
    as the Light of the World.
May we place all our trust in his guidance
    as we seek our way in life.
Amen.

Quotation of the week

It takes two sides to make a lasting peace, but it only takes one to make the first step. (Edward Kennedy)

Alternative reading

2 Corinthians 5; 17-21

• 17th March

St Patrick, Apostle of Ireland
It was Patrick, the patron saint of Ireland, who took the Christian Faith to Ireland, and established it there by his own courage and holiness of life.

Prayer of the day

God our Father,
    you sent St Patrick
    as a missionary to Ireland;
    may we too be your missionaries
    showing everyone, by our lives,
    that you are a God of goodness and love.
Amen.

• 19th March

St Joseph, Husband of Mary
Joseph was the husband of Mary and the foster-father of Jesus. He was a village carpenter by trade. He is now the patron of the Catholic Church.

Prayer of the day

Almighty Father,
    you entrusted your Son into the care of St Joseph.
May his prayers help us to be caring
    and worthy of trust.
Amen.

Prayers this week

For our parents, especially our mothers, who have done so much for us; we pray for their good health and happiness.

Fifth Week
of Lent (C)

Theme

Trying again

The idea of stoning a woman to death because she had been unfaithful to her husband (this week's reading) seems very barbaric to us (thankfully Jesus saved her) but it shows that people in those days had clear and firm standards and values – something many people don't have today. Jesus told the woman, 'Go and don't sin any more'. She was given the chance to make a fresh start. This is the message of Lent; if we are really sorry, God will forgive us and we can start afresh, try again.

Reading of the week

John 8:1-11

Prayer of the week

Father in heaven
the love of your Son led him to accept
the suffering of the cross.
Change our selfishness into self-giving.
Help us to transform the darkness of this world's pain
into the life and joy of Easter.
Amen.

Quotation of the week

We die daily. Happy those who daily come to live as well.
(George Macdonald)

Alternative reading

Philippians 3:8-14

• 25th March

The Annunciation of the Lord
Mary, the young girl of Nazareth, is asked to be the mother of the Christ; she accepts. This event is nine months from Christmas Day and is the origin of Mother's Day, being the day on which Mary conceived by the special power of God.

Prayer of the day

God our Father,
your Son became man
and was born of the Virgin Mary.
May we remember and thank God
for our own mothers
at this time of the year.
Amen.

Prayers this week

For our parents, especially our mothers, who have done, and are doing, so much for us. We pray for their good health and happiness.

Assembly idea

This week's Gospel story is easily dramatised and can involve a flexible number of pupils. They can make 'stones' out of screwed-up waste paper (but they will have to be reminded that they never actually get a chance to throw them!). If an alb is available Jesus could wear this to distinguish him from the others.

Second Week of Easter (C)

Theme

Community of faith

If you are being asked to believe something which seems to be impossible then your doubts seem very reasonable. Thomas knew Jesus was dead, very dead from crucifixion; so it was natural for him to say, 'Unless I put my finger into the wounds . . . I will not believe'. When he too sees Jesus, risen and with them again, he is convinced. For two thousand years the Christian community has based its faith on witnesses like Thomas. His doubting was important for us.

Reading of the week   John 20:19-31

Prayer of the week

Heavenly Father and God of Mercy,
    we do not look for Jesus among the dead,
    for he is alive.
Increase our faith that we may believe
    without looking for evidence first.
May our faith and trust grow every day. Amen.

Quotation of the week   Belief is a truth held in the mind. Faith is a fire in the heart. (J. Newton)

Alternative readings

Acts 2:42-47
1 Peter 1:3-9

• 16th April

St Bernadette of Lourdes
At the age of 14 (in 1858) the simple peasant girl Marie Bernard (nicknamed Bernadette) was amazed to be chosen to be the recipient of a series of apparitions of the Virgin Mary at the Grotto at Lourdes. She became a saint not on the strength of this, but as a result of the heroism of her later life. She is remembered by the millions of pilgrims, young and old, who go to Lourdes every year.

Prayer of the day

Lord, we see the wonder of your love
    in the saintly life of Bernadette and her witness to Christ.
May her example inspire us
    to love Christ faithfully in our own lives. Amen.

Prayers this week   For people who find it very difficult to believe in Christ's resurrection.

Assembly idea

Brief six pupils to think up remarks like: 'I don't believe you because it's rubbish'; 'It's stupid to believe that, it couldn't happen'; 'You can't believe what you can't prove'. (They are not allowed to shout or be rude.) Brief another suitable pupil to stand at the front to make a little speech about how, for example, white frogs can now be seen in rivers and ponds. The speaker is surrounded – not too close – by the other six as she delivers her speech, and they continually interrupt. Stop after a few minutes. Make the point that the Church has been speaking about the Resurrection of Jesus for 2,000 years and has been constantly shouted down; but it has never given up and continues.

Third Week
of Easter (C)

Theme

Living witnesses

It is a remarkable claim; that your friend has risen from the dead! No wonder that the friends of Jesus, at first, found it difficult to believe. As soon as they did, they were keen to tell everyone they met about it! Each Apostle died for that keenness and that witnessing. All Christians are faced with the same challenge; to believe that Jesus rose from the dead and to witness to that belief by a life of joy and hope.

Reading of the week   John 21:1-19

Prayer of the week

Father, you raised your Son
   to a glorious new life with you.
May we have a deep faith in the Resurrection
   and be your witnesses by the joy
   and quality of our lives.
Amen.

Quotation of the week

Our Lord has written the promise of the Resurrection, not in books alone, but in every leaf in springtime. (Martin Luther)

Alternative readings

Acts 5:27-32, 40-41
Acts 7:54-60

• 1st May

St Joseph, Husband of Our Lady; Patron of all workers
Jesus was a manual worker, like his foster-father, Joseph; both knew the hard daily grind of manual work. For this reason the Church has always supported trade unions and campaigned for just and fair working conditions for all workers. St Joseph was declared the patron saint of workers in 1955.

Prayer of the day

God our Father, creator of the Universe,
   you call us to use our gifts and talents
   to work with you for the development
   and improvement of our world.
Help us to find satisfying work that will benefit
   not only ourselves but others.
Amen.

Prayers this week

For those who, in our world, earn so little that they cannot even feed themselves and their families properly.

Assembly idea

Write the word 'witness' on the board and ask what we would be expected to do if we were called as a witness in a court. (Answer: tell truthfully what you know about an event or person.) The friends of Jesus told everyone what they had seen with their own eyes; for them the risen Jesus was a fact. They had spoken to him; he was no ghost because they also ate with him. Our faith is based on their witnessing.

Fourth Week of Easter (C)

Week of Prayer for Vocations

Theme

The Good Shepherd

Lollipop ladies we see, guiding children safely across the road. Shepherds we don't see, but their job was very similar. At the time of Jesus a shepherd was a tough outdoor man, who led mixed herds of sheep and goats which wandered stupidly all over the place. Jesus said, 'I am the good shepherd' – who cares for us, his mixed herd. Following our good shepherd can give real meaning and direction to our lives.

Reading of the week

John 10:11-16

Prayer of the week

Almighty and caring God,
    your Son called himself the Good Shepherd.
May we follow our shepherd with courage
    especially when we are mocked
      for being Christians and his friends.
Amen.

Quotation of the week

The wolf eats oft of the sheep that have been warned. (English proverb)

Alternative reading

John 10:1-6

Prayers this week

For young people who are mocked and ridiculed for being churchgoers; and all who are persecuted for their beliefs.

Assembly idea

Write on the board 'Crossing lady' or 'Lollipop man' (whichever applies locally). Ask for suggestions of others who care for people. If they do not add 'shepherd' then suggest it, with suitable comment about caring for others, and having the courage to live by your beliefs.

Fifth Week
of Easter (C)

Theme

Love one another

Jesus says, 'I've got a new and simple rule for you; love one another, just as I have loved you.' It is simple and clear, but it is difficult because it clashes with our own selfish love. We find it easier to push in front of others, grab the best place or part for ourselves, take rather than give, expect to be waited upon rather than serve. Jesus is right, though: real, lasting happiness and maturity come from giving, not taking.

Reading of the week

John 13:31-35

Prayer of the week

God our Father,
   look upon us with love.
You have made us your children by Baptism
    and given us our Lord Jesus Christ
    as our model and guide.
Help us to live lovingly
    as we faithfully follow such a wonderful friend.
Amen.

Quotation of the week

The love of our neighbour is the only door out of the prison of self. (George Macdonald)

Alternative readings

1 John 3:1-3
1 John 4:7-21

Prayers this week

For people who feel any form of hatred for others, that they may find real peace from learning to love and accept others.

Assembly idea

Prepare six large sheets of paper. On one side write the letters of 'L-o-v-e i-s'; on the reverse (in the same order, so C on back of L) write 'C-a-r-i-n-g'. Give sheets to six volunteers (only the words 'Love is' should be shown). In line the six pupils reveal the words 'Love is'. Ask for suggestions, which Jesus would approve of, to complete the sentence. After a number of ideas the letters on the reverse are shown. Explain that Jesus asks us to *love*, which is not the same as *like*; it means the same as *caring*.

Sixth Week
of Easter (C)

Theme

The peace of Christ

It's great to feel 'all-together', at peace with ourselves. Peace comes from inside us, from feeling good about ourselves and knowing that all our relationships, with family, friends, the people we meet each day – and God – are in good working order. In other words we have a good conscience about everything. We can get and keep such a wonderful sense of peace if we remain close to Christ in friendship; then we share in his peace.

Reading of the week

John 14:23-29

Prayer of the week

Ever-living God,
    fill us with the Spirit
    of your truth, love and peace.
Help us to live by the truth
    and enjoy the peace that only you can give.
Amen.

Quotation of the week

Where there is peace, God is. (George Herbert)

Alternative readings

John 20:19-23
1 Thessalonians 5:16-23

• Thursday

The Ascension of the Lord
The 'Going-up' or 'Ascension' of Christ brings to an end his appearances to his friends after the Resurrection. What happened on the first Ascension day is a little mysterious, but for believers it is the *promise* that matters: the promise that as Jesus lives now with his Father, so, after death, shall we; the promise that there *is* life after death.

Prayer of the day

Father in heaven,
    our thoughts turn to the reality
    of everlasting life with you,
    when we recall Christ's Ascension.
May we, one day, follow where he has led,
    and find our hope in his glory.
Amen.

Prayers this week

For people who are tormented by depression and have no peace of mind. For those who work with the mentally ill.

Assembly idea

On five A4 sheets of plain white paper write the letters P, E, A, C and E. On the reverse of P, write 'people'; on E write 'everywhere'; on A write 'appreciate'; on C 'calm'; and on E 'environment'. Have five pupils at the front and, after a few words on how we all need peace and quiet in our lives and time for reflection, ask the pupils to show the word 'Peace'; then after a moment turn their sheets over. Follow with a minute of silent reflection and close with the *Prayer of the week*.

Seventh Week
of Easter (C)

Week of Prayer
for the Media

Theme

One with God

A couple in love want to be together all the time; they want to be close to one another. A condemned man's final words to his friends before execution are very precious. We have part of the final speech of Jesus, just hours before his execution, as this week's reading. Those words are precious to us. He pleads with God to keep us, his friends, close to him even after death.

Reading of the week

John 17:20-26

Prayer of the week

Father, help us always to keep in mind
   how precious we are to you.
Fill us with your Spirit
   that we may show your love to others
   and give glory to your name.
Amen.

Alternative readings

John 3:16-21
John 15:1-8

Quotation of the week

The seed of God is in us. Pear seeds grow into pear trees, nut seeds into nut trees, and God seeds into God. (Eckhart)

Assembly ideas

1 *World Communications Week*
The Church is concerned that the media and all forms of world communication should be used to promote what is good and not promote evil of any kind. Bring in a newspaper and ask why papers seem to report only bad news. Pray for journalists, TV news editors, etc.

2 *Month of May*
For centuries the month of May has been dedicated to Mary, the Mother of Jesus. Before the Reformation our country was known as 'The Dowry of Mary'. May processions and the reciting of the rosary in special services were once features of Catholic May. Explain this and use the 'Hail Mary'. A rosary might be shown and a decade said with the form.

Prayers this week

For those who work in the media, especially for editors responsible for presenting the news.

Feast of
the Holy Trinity (C)

Gospel: John 16:12-15

Theme

Glory to the Father, the Son and the Holy Spirit

On Sunday, around the world, all Christians celebrated the belief in the divine 'family' of the Godhead: three persons in one unity (Tri-unity) of being. This belief is unique to all Christians. It is impossible to imagine and very difficult to understand, but it is an essential belief for the Christian faith. The *Father*, who created everything, gave us the *Son* (or 'the *Word*') who rescued us and gave us his *Spirit*, the Spirit of faith, hope and love.

Reading of the week   John 16:12-15

Prayer of the week

Father, you sent us your Son
   to bring us the truth,
   and your Spirit to make us holy.
Through them we come to know
   the mystery of your life.
Help us to worship you,
   Father, Son and Holy Spirit.
Amen.

• 27th May

St Augustine: first Archbishop of Canterbury
Augustine was a reluctant missionary, accompanied by 40 other Benedictine monks who, 1,400 years ago, landed near Ramsgate and set about converting the people of Kent to Christianity. He converted the King of Kent and became the first Archbishop of Canterbury.

• Thursday

The Body and Blood of Christ (The Feast of Corpus Christi)
Just as in our human life we need food and drink, so in our spiritual life we need Christ to nourish and sustain us. He feeds us with himself, with his words, through Scripture; and with the Sacrament of his Body and his Blood. As we eat together the sacred bread and wine, we share with one another, and so the community is made strong as we grow personally in strength.

Prayer of the day

Lord Jesus Christ,
   we believe that you live among us
   and we worship your presence
   in the sacrament of your Body and Blood.
May the same Body and Blood give us strength
   to live the Christian life faithfully.
Amen.

Prayers this week

For those who work for Christian unity so that soon all may share the same sacrament at the altar of Christ.

Theme

God has no favourites

Although nurses in a hospital ward may have their preferences, they cannot pick and choose whom they will look after; they must treat everyone equally. God is even better than that, he actually *loves* every person equally, and loves everyone the same. Christians do not get more love and care than Muslims or Sikhs or people who sincerely cannot believe in God. Colour, class, gender mean nothing to God.

Reading of the week

Luke 7:1-10

Prayer of the week

Father, your love never fails.
You offer it to every person you have created;
   social class, colour and gender
   mean nothing to you;
May they mean nothing to us,
   as we offer your love to all.
Amen.

Quotation of the week

Before God and the bus driver we are all equal. (German proverb)

Alternative readings

Galatians 3:26-28
1 Kings 8:41-43

• Friday

The Sacred Heart of Jesus (Gospel: Luke 15:3-7)
Cards with hearts on are sent on Valentine's Day; the human heart is recognised as a symbol of love. The symbol of the heart of Jesus stands for that amazing love he had for us which took him to the cross where his heart was pierced.

Prayer of the day

Father, we rejoice in all the gifts of love
   we have received,
   and especially for the wonderful love
   of Jesus our Lord and Saviour.
Teach us to show that love
   by love-filled service to our brothers and sisters.
Amen.

Alternative readings

Romans 5:5-11
1 John 4:7-16

Prayers this week

For any of our school community, and their families, who are prejudiced against others because of their colour, religion or class.

Assembly idea

Write the words 'Racism', 'Sexism' and 'Ageism' on the board and ask what Jesus would have to say about these words.

Tenth Week
in Ordinary Time (C)

Theme

Compassion

We so often hear sad stories about very sick people, and we feel like helping in some way. The word 'compassion' comes from two Latin words, *cum passio*, which means 'suffering with'. When, like Jesus, in this week's Gospel story, we feel for someone, we *suffer with* them; we show compassion and say things like, 'Just let me know if there's anything I can do': there is always one thing we can do, and that is to pray.

Reading of the week

Luke 7:11-17

Prayer of the week

God of wisdom and love,
    from you all goodness comes;
    help us to show your love and goodness
    to those in need, as your Son did.
Amen.

Alternative readings

1 Kings 17:17-24
Mark 2:1-12

• 13th June

St Anthony of Padua, Doctor of the Church
Many people ask St Anthony to help them find things that they have lost. In real life Anthony was a famous preacher of the thirteenth century, and a follower of St Francis. He is usually shown in pictures or in statues holding the child Jesus; that is because in a vision he saw the child Jesus. (See also Year A, page 130)

Quotation from St Anthony
He prays best who does not know that he is praying.

Prayer of the day

Almighty God,
    you have given St Anthony to us
    as a ready helper in time of need.
With his assistance
    may we follow Christ more faithfully.
Amen.

Prayers this week

For all those who are incurably sick, lonely and housebound.

Assembly idea

Invite a group of pupils to think about the opening paragraph. In two contrasting playlets or role-plays, performed side-by-side or one after the other, illustrate a person for whom we might feel little compassion – for example, a violent thug who hurts himself – and one for whom we *would* feel compassion – like a young person terminally ill with cancer.

Eleventh Week
in Ordinary Time (C)

Theme

Forgiveness

The three most difficult words to say are 'I am sorry'. The Church is for people who need to say those words, and do say them, to God and to those they have offended. The Church is for sinners. Jesus was told off many times by respectable people for spending time with the gamblers, drug addicts and prostitutes of his time. Christ showed real concern; love can wipe out wrong-doing.

Reading of the week

Luke 7:36-50

Prayer of the week

God of wisdom and love,
    from you all goodness comes;
    help us, who have done wrong,
    to return to a life of thoughtfulness and love.
Amen.

Alternative reading

2 Samuel 12:7-10, 13 (It will be necessary to fill in the background to this reading.)

• 20th June

St Alban, Britain's first martyr
A citizen of fourth-century Verulam who was converted to Christianity and, for sheltering a priest, was executed in place of the priest who escaped. An abbey to St Alban was built on the site and Verulam became the modern town of St Albans.

Prayer of the day

Father, you gave your martyr Alban
    the courage to die for Christ and his Gospel.
Give us the humility to believe
    and the courage to admit to others
      that we are Christians.
Amen.

• 22nd June

St John Fisher and St Thomas More, English martyrs
John Fisher was the Bishop of Rochester, Kent, who stood up for the Catholic Church (the Old Faith of this country) against King Henry VIII and was beheaded for the faith. Thomas More was the Chancellor of England who also opposed Henry and was beheaded on Tower Hill.

Quotation from St Thomas
Occupy your minds with good thoughts or the enemy will fill it with bad.

Prayer of the day

Father, may the example
    of John Fisher and Thomas More,
    give us the courage to proclaim
    our faith by the witness of our lives.
Amen.

Prayers this week

For those who are miserable because they cannot forgive others and nurture resentment and hate.

Twelfth Week
in Ordinary Time (C)

Theme

Equality

The rich are not better than the poor; men are not better than women. Jesus treated everyone equally. St Paul repeated this teaching and developed it: 'There is no distinction between slave and freeman, male and female; all of you are one in Christ Jesus.' There is no room for any form of discrimination by Christ's followers in a Christian community like ours.

Reading of the week

Luke 9:18-24

Prayer of the week

Loving Father,
   you are the guide and protector of all your people,
   female and male, poor and rich;
   whatever our situation or role in life,
   be always near, for we place all our trust in you.
Amen.

Quotation of the week

All animals are equal but some animals are more equal than others. (George Orwell)

Alternative reading

Romans 8:12-17

• 29th June

Feast of St Peter and St Paul
The Christian Church was founded by the faith and leadership of Peter, and the hard missionary work of Paul. They are the two foundation stones, after Christ himself, of the Christian Church.

Prayer of the day

God our Father,
   today we joyfully celebrate
   the feast of the apostles, Peter and Paul.
Through them and their efforts
   your Church first received the faith;
   keep us faithful to their teaching.
Amen.

Prayers this week

For women who are victims of discrimination and all who suffer from the evils of Racism.

Assembly idea

Draw a large heart on the board (red, if possible). Ask what this symbol has to do with our theme this week. Accept suggestions. Answer: this is the symbol of love, and love unites us all. It knows no boundaries, no distinctions; it is the same for rich or poor/male or female/black or white/one religion or another. At the end of life Christ the judge will not notice if we are male or female, rich or poor; he will only want to know how loving we have been.

Thirteenth Week
in Ordinary Time (C)

Theme

Commitment

Marriage is not popular with modern youth, it is said, because they are frightened of making a commitment. Placing our faith in another is what is asked for when we commit ourselves to them. Jesus asks us for just such a commitment and asks us to place our faith in him. If we can learn to trust Christ perhaps that will help us to trust others who profess their love of us.

Reading of the week

Luke 9:51-62

Prayer of the day

Loving Father,
    you call us to commit ourselves to you
    in the name of your Son.
Give us the courage to live the Christian life
    and accept the friendship of Christ.
Amen.

Quotation of the week

Give me such love for God and men as will blot out all hatred and bitterness. (Dietrich Bonhoeffer)

Alternative reading

Galatians 5:13-18

• 1st July

St Oliver Plunkett, martyr
Oliver was the last Catholic to die for his faith in London, at Tyburn, in 1681. At his death he was the Archbishop of Armagh, Ireland; no Irish judge would convict him, so he was sent to an English court, where he was found guilty of 'propagating the Catholic Religion'.

Prayer of the day

Almighty God,
    your martyr Oliver died for his Catholic faith.
May we cherish the same faith
    and be faithful to it in life, as he was in death.
Amen.

Prayers this week

For ourselves that we may be true to any commitment we make to others.

Assembly idea

If you have a wedding or engagement ring, show it to the form and ask what it is a sign of. (Answer: a commitment to another person.) Alternatively, show a picture of a Religious sister and ask the same question about her habit. Follow with a prayer for all those in our school community who have made a lifelong commitment.

Fourteenth Week
in Ordinary Time (C)

Theme

The peace of Christ

We are whole persons; if we are upset or in mental turmoil it affects our whole life: how we eat, sleep and relate to people. That is not having peace. If we keep our friendship with Christ alive and live as he asks ('love one another as I have loved you') then we will have peace of mind.

Readings of the week

Galatians 6:14-18
Isaiah 66:10-14

Prayer of the week

Father of peace,
   you gave us your Son
   that we may find and live in peace.
May we grow in love
   and share that love with others,
   so that we may always live in peace.
Amen.

Alternative readings

James 3:13-18
Philippians 4:4-9

• 11th July

St Benedict, Patron of Europe (European Feast)
Benedict and his followers, the Benedictine monks, did more to advance Christian values and quality of life throughout Europe than any other person or group. Benedict died in 547 but the hundreds of monasteries have continued his work of education and the spread of culture right up to today.

Quotation from St Benedict
Idleness is the enemy of the soul.

Prayer of the day

God our Father,
   you made St Benedict
   an outstanding educator and guide
   to show people how they should live in dignity and peace.
Grant that, like him,
   we may prefer your love to anything else.
Amen.

Prayers this week

For our Church schools that, in the tradition of St Benedict, they may be centres of excellence, discipline and hospitality.

Assembly idea

Give out slips of paper to each member of the form. Ask them to think of someone (only one person) in the form whom they rarely speak to, don't get on with, or have recently fallen out with. They write a simple message which must include the word 'peace'; it can be as simple as 'Peace be with you'. They fold the paper twice and put the person's name on the front. Collect all the slips and deliver them. (Caution is required if deep animosity exists in the form.)

Fifteenth Week
in Ordinary Time (C)

Theme

Love your neighbour

Again and again we return to this theme, because it is at the centre of Jesus' teaching and it is difficult to achieve. At the end of another school year it is good to remind ourselves that no matter where we are – at home, or school or away on holiday – this command of Jesus always applies. If we centre our lives on these words we will never be without friends, we will always be respected, and we will always find true happiness.

Reading of the week

Luke 10:25-37

Prayer of the week

God our Father,
  your Son showed us how to live happy lives.
May we follow his commandment,
  and love and respect others.
We ask this through Christ,
  our Friend and Saviour.
Amen.

Alternative readings

John 13:2-15
1 John 3:11-18

• 25th July

St James, Apostle
James, and his brother John, were fishermen when Jesus called them to be among his followers. After the resurrection of Jesus, James became the leader of the Christians in Jerusalem (he was the first bishop there). He was arrested by King Herod Agrippa and beheaded in 42.

Quotation from St James:
Be quick to listen, slow to speak, and slow to become angry.

Prayer of the day

Almighty Father,
  by the martyrdom of St James
  you blessed the work of the early Church.
May his courage give us encouragement
  and his prayers give us strength
  to be faithful to our faith.
Amen.

Prayers this week

For every member of our form, that they may all have a good, safe and happy holiday.

Assembly idea

Provide pieces of paper and ask each pupil to take the addresses of three members of the form whom they will definitely not see in the coming six weeks, and promise to send them a postcard from holiday.

Part Three

End of Year C/Beginning of Year A

The Year of Luke's Gospel (C)
The Year of Matthew's Gospel (A)

Twenty-second Week
in Ordinary Time (C)

Theme — *Humility*

Our themes each week are suggested by the readings used at Mass on the first day of the week, Sunday. The same readings, and often the same theme, are used all around the Catholic world. From headteacher to youngest pupil, we are loved equally by God, and we owe everything that we have to that same loving God. There is no place in a Christian community for arrogant pride. There will be none if we all realise that our individual gifts and talents are from God, for the service of others.

Reading of the week — Luke 14:1-14

Prayer of the week — Almighty Father,
    as we begin a new year,
    fill our hearts with love of you,
    that we may find happiness
    by following the rule of love
    your Son Jesus Christ gave us to live by.
Amen.

Quotation of the week — Humility is the truth about ourselves loved. (C. Carey-Elwes)

Alternative reading — Ecclesiasticus 3:17-20, 28-29

• 8th September — *The Birthday of Our Lady*
We do not know the actual date or day of Mary's birth, but just as we keep our Queen Elizabeth's official birthday so we have this day to celebrate the Queen of Heaven. All birthdays are celebrations of life, so today we thank God for the life of Mary, the mother of Jesus.

Prayer of the day — Merciful Father,
    the birth of Jesus brought a promise
    of peace to our world.
May today's celebration
    of the birthday of Mary, his mother,
    bring us closer
    to a perfect and lasting peace.
Amen.

Prayers this week — For all our new pupils and students, especially in Year 7.

Assembly idea — Write on the board: 'Who is the most important person in this school'. (Leave out the question mark.) Ask for suggestions and write these on the board. After a minute or two ask if it is any different if we add the words 'to God'. (Answer: of course; God loves us all equally, so we are all equally important in his eyes.)

Twenty-third Week in Ordinary Time (C)

Theme

Being a Christian

The Catholic school has been called 'an oasis'; a place, in the desert of this world, where people can experience the loving care and values taught by Jesus. Often, in our cities, life is hard and dangerous but the Catholic school should strive to be a community where there are different, higher values; where each unique God-loved individual is accepted with love. Being a Christian community makes a difference, or it isn't Christian and Catholic.

Reading of the week

Luke 14:25-33

Prayer of the week

God our Father,
    draw us into the circle
    of your life and love,
    that our eyes may be opened
    to the wonders of this life that you give us,
    and our hearts to one another. Amen.

Quotation of the week

To live in prayer together is to walk in love together.
(Margaret Moore Jacobs)

Alternative readings

Ephesians 6:10-18
Ephesians 1:15-18

• 14th September

The Triumph of the Cross
The symbol of the cross is *the* Christian sign, marked on our foreheads at Baptism and used each time before we pray to remind us of Baptism. It is the sign of love: of Christ's tremendous love and victory over death.

Prayer of the day

God our Father,
    in his love and obedience to you
    your Son accepted death on a cross.
May that cross be for us a sign of love
    obedience and forgiveness. Amen.

• 15th September

Our Lady of Sorrows
As Jesus died on the cross his mother stood there with the other women. In her unspeakable sorrow she gave comfort, by her presence, to her dying son.

Prayer of the day

Father, as your Son died on the cross
    his mother Mary stood by him,
    sharing his sufferings.
May we stand by those who suffer
    and bring them comfort. Amen.

Prayers this week

For our school, that it may be recognised by all as a community of love where Christ's values are taught and lived.

Twenty-fourth Week in Ordinary Time (C)

Theme

Forgiving one another

One of the most difficult things to say is 'I'm sorry'. In what Jesus said and did he showed how important it is to say 'sorry'. He prayed, 'Father, forgive them', as he hung on the cross. This week we have Jesus' story about the father who forgave his son. God, our loving Father, will always forgive us, but there are two conditions: we must be sincere and we must forgive other people who have hurt us.

Reading of the week

Luke 15: 11-32

Prayer of the week

Almighty God,
    there are times when we need to return to you
    and ask forgiveness.
May we offer the same love and forgiveness
    to those who hurt us.
Amen.

Quotation of the week

There's no point in burying a hatchet if you're going to put up a marker on the site. (Sydney Harris)

Alternative readings

1 Timothy 1:12-17
Exodus 32:7-11, 13-14

• 21st September

St Matthew, Apostle and Gospel writer
Matthew (or Levi) was a hated tax collector who, when called by Jesus, left everything to follow him. The Gospel attributed to him arose from his courageous preaching of the Good News.

Prayer of the day

God of mercy,
    you chose an unpopular tax collector, Matthew,
    to share the dignity of the Apostles.
By his example and prayers
    help us to follow and be faithful to Christ.
Amen.

Prayers this week

For those who are so full of bitterness that they cannot offer forgiveness to those who have hurt them.

Assembly idea

The Gospel story of the Lost Son is ideal for dramatising, or a dramatic reading, in the form room, with parts from the *Dramatised Bible*.

Twenty-fifth Week in Ordinary Time (C)

Theme

On the side of the poor

One child dies every eight seconds on our planet from hunger or hunger-related diseases. That must concern Christ; he was always on the side of the poor. He knew what it was to be poor. Jesus was born in someone else's stable and buried in another man's grave. All Christ's followers today are called to speak up for the poor. In a rich nation like ours we have a special responsibility to share what we have with God's poor.

Reading this week

Amos 8:4-7

Prayer of the week

Father, guide us, as you guide creation
    according to your law of love.
Fill us with your own generous love
    that we may find this love in each other
    as we help and support one another. Amen.

Quotation of the week

Must the hunger become anger and the anger become fury before anything will be done? (John Steinbeck)

Alternative readings

James 2:14-17
2 Corinthians 8:1-9

• 27th September

St Vincent de Paul
Vincent lived in France just over 300 years ago when there were many cruel and unjust practices. Vincent was a model of generosity; although a priest he offered to take the place of galley slaves (who rowed big boats) and took the poor into his home. His work continues today through the Sisters of Charity and the SVP Society found in many parishes.

Prayer of the day

God our Father,
    you gave Vincent the courage and strength
    to work for the poor.
Help us to show the same concern and care
    for anyone in need. Amen.

• 29th September

Saints Michael, Gabriel and Raphael, archangels
An angel is a spiritual 'messenger' from God; archangels are very special messengers. So, for example, Gabriel brought God's message about the birth of John the Baptist and of Jesus. The whole spiritual realm of God's spirits is celebrated today.

Prayer of the week

God our Father,
    may those who serve you constantly in heaven
    keep our lives safe from all harm. Amen.

Prayers this week

For the work of the aid agencies, especially CAFOD.

Twenty-sixth Week in Ordinary Time (C)

Theme

Sharing what we have

At this time of the year, all around our country, there are Harvest festivals; people thanking God for food and all the good things that they enjoy. But we live in an unfair world and throughout the Bible there are warnings: 'Look out, you who are rich . . . and exploit the poor.' No one can genuinely love God and ignore the poor; a very real test of being good, in God's eyes, is a willingness to share what we have.

Readings of the week

Luke 16:19-31
Amos 6:1, 4-7

Prayer of the week

Father of unlimited goodness,
    thank you for all your gifts
    which make our lives comfortable.
May we show the same generosity
    to your people who are in need. Amen.

Quotation of the week

Whoever stops his ears to the poor shall cry himself and not be heard. (Hebrew proverb)

Alternative readings

Amos 8:4-7
Matthew 25:31-46

• 1st October

St Thérèse of Lisieux
Thérèse was only 24 when she died in 1897, after being a Carmelite sister for nine years. She never went anywhere and few people knew her while she lived, but she is today one of the most famous female saints. How? Because she learned how to make everything in her life a prayer, an act of love for God. (She is a lovely person to learn more about.)

Prayer of the day

God our Father,
    you promised eternal happiness
    to those who live simply and trustfully
    like little children.
Help us to follow the way of St Thérèse
    who lived just like that. Amen.

• 4th October

St Francis of Assisi
Francis is remembered today for his love of animals; but in his own time and for most of history he was known as 'the poor man of Assisi'. He gave all his possessions, even his clothes, to the poor.

Prayer of the day

Father, you helped St Francis to live
    and work for the poor.
May we follow his example
    and show the same caring love. Amen.

Prayers this week

For the homeless families of our own neighbourhood and those who sleep on the streets of our towns and cities.

Twenty-seventh Week in Ordinary Time (C)

Theme

Faith

Before catching the bus to school in the morning you do not first ask the driver if he can drive! You trust that he can; you have faith in him. Without trust and faith we cannot live. We build our lives on such trust. Our faith in God and his loving care grows daily if we ask him to increase our faith; if we develop it by praying regularly.

Reading of the week

Luke 17:5-10

Prayer of the week

Almighty and eternal God,
   your love for us surpasses all our hopes and desires.
Help us to place our total confidence in you,
   that anxieties may not cloud our minds,
   and we may think only of your love
   and the love we should have for others.
Amen.

Quotation of the week

I do not want merely to possess a faith; I want a faith that possesses me.
(Charles Kingsley)

Alternative reading

Hebrews 11:1-3, 8-10

• 13th October

St Edward the Confessor, King of England
Edward's concern for the poor was legendary and he refounded the Abbey of Westminster where he is buried. He is called 'Confessor' because he witnessed to Christ by the way he lived, and this distinguishes him from St Edward the Martyr who witnessed by his death.

Prayer of the day

Almighty Father,
   your servant, Edward, king of England,
   showed real concern for the poor.
May we imitate him in our desire
   to help the homeless of our big cities.
Amen.

Prayers this week

For people who have no faith in anything and find life aimless and without meaning and purpose.

Assembly idea

Put the words 'Faith can move mountains' on the board and ask for ideas as to its meaning. (The word 'mountain' is, of course, used metaphorically to refer to a great 'pile' of worries and anxieties. So if a person places complete faith and trust in God, that mound of anxiety can be removed.)

Twenty-eighth Week in Ordinary Time (C)

Theme

Giving thanks

'I know what I want and I want it now' sums up so many people's attitude, even if they are Christians and pray. Christians, however, are supposed to be God's 'thank-you' people. The central prayer of our faith is called the 'Eucharist' which means the 'Thanksgiving'. A truly Christian life is full of joy and thanksgiving to God for all his goodness each day.

Reading of the week

Luke 17:11-19

Prayer of the week

Father, the hand of your loving kindness
    powerfully but gently guides
    all the moments of our day.
Give us the gift of the same loving kindness,
    that we may treat everyone with love and respect
    today and every day.
Amen.

Quotation of the week

The thankful heart is the only door that opens to God. (Joe Orton)

Alternative reading

Colossians 3:15-17

• 18th October

St Luke, Gospel writer
Luke never knew Jesus personally; he was the travelling companion of St Paul and heard the Gospel from him. Luke was an educated man, a doctor, and he researched the Good News before recording it. His principal aim was to make clear that the Good News was for everyone, women as well as men, the poor as well as the rich.

Prayer of the day

Father, you chose St Luke
    to reveal by his preaching and writing
    the mystery of your love for the poor.
May everyone come to understand
    that Christ's Good News is for all.
Amen.

Prayers this week

For the carers who give their lives to the nursing of disabled, handicapped and housebound relatives.

Assembly idea

Ask, 'When as a child you left a party, what did you say?' 'Thank you for having me'? If we say 'thank you' for the few hours of a short party, what should we say to God for a whole day, or a whole week? God our Father likes us to say 'thank you'.

Twenty-ninth Week
in Ordinary Time (C)

Theme

Keep praying

Prayer is like oxygen for the Christian. There can be no life without it. If you love someone you want to be with them, talk to them, share your ideas and thoughts with them. If you love God, if Christ is your friend, then it is natural to want to talk to him. It is not always easy to love and share, and it is not always easy to pray, but God will always help the willing person and reward every effort.

Reading of the week

Luke 18:1-8

Prayer of the week

Lord our God, Father of all,
    you guard us, keep us safe
    and know our most secret thoughts.
Inspire us to speak frequently to you in prayer,
    so that our relationship with you
    will grow and develop.
Amen.

Quotation of the week

Prayer enlarges the heart until it is capable of containing God's gift of himself. (Mother Teresa)

Alternative reading

Exodus 17:8-13
2 Timothy 3:14-4:2

Prayers this week

For those who dedicate their lives to spreading Christ's Good News in foreign lands.

Assembly idea

Ask, 'If you want to pray, is it necessary to close your eyes, fold your hands and kneel down?' Response will probably be mixed. Pick up the suggestions that no special posture, place or words are necessary. It's the thought or words that count. Ask if there is a pupil who has someone that he/she would like the group to pray for.

Thirtieth Week
in Ordinary Time (C)

Theme

Dependence on God

Most people try to live their lives without taking any notice of God. Then they wonder why life doesn't seem to have any meaning and they can never find satisfaction or even peace and happiness. Our Gospel reading shows that arrogance and contempt for others are rejected by God; simple, humble dependence – realising that everything comes from God and that we need him – brings peace and true happiness.

Reading of the week   Luke 18:9-14

Prayer of the week

Almighty and ever-living God,
    strengthen and deepen our love,
    that we may learn to love you
    in all we do for our neighbours,
    family and friends. Amen.

Quotation of the week   God is faithful, and if we serve him faithfully he will provide for all our needs. (St Richard of Chichester)

Alternative reading   Ecclesiasticus 35:12-14, 16-19

• 1st November

All Saints' Day
Big families like to get together sometimes. The Christian family includes those who have died and are with God (we call this 'heaven'). Today we remember all the good members of our individual families who have died and, we believe, are with God. They are saints and we ask them to speak to God for us.

Prayer of the day

Father, all-powerful and ever-living God,
    today we rejoice in all the holy men and women
    of every time and place.
May their prayers bring us the help we need
    to be faithful to you. Amen.

• 2nd November

All Souls' Day
Not everyone in our family (both our individual families and the family of Christians) gets to heaven immediately. Some people are left for a while to prepare for being with God. Today we pray that all our relatives who have died may soon join that part of the Christian family that is with God.

Prayer of the day

Merciful Father,
    please hear our prayers.
May all those who have died
    be taken up into your wonderful and merciful love. Amen.

Prayers this week   For all the deceased members of our families.

Thirty-first Week in Ordinary Time (C)

Theme

Accepting one another

We each need to be loved and accepted by others. An 'isolate' who feels unwanted is a desperately sad figure. In our Gospel story Zacchaeus is an 'isolate', alone up his tree and hated for being a tax collector. Jesus notices him and visits his home. That's the example that we must try to follow. We must accept people as they are, not as we would want them to be; no one in our community should feel isolated and unwanted.

Reading of the week

Luke 19:1-10

Prayer of the week

Almighty and ever-living God,
   strengthen our faith, hope and love.
Help us to grow in love
   and show real concern and care
   for all those we live and work with.
Amen.

Quotation of the week

Have a deaf ear for unkind remarks about others, and a blind eye to their trivial faults. (Sir Walter Scott)

Alternative reading

Wisdom 11:22-12:2

• Time of Remembrance

God lives outside all time; the past and the future are *present* to God. So all those we love, who have left this life, are *present* to God; they are as much in his presence as we are. We remember them with affection; they are actually present to the loving God, our Father, even now as we think of them.

Prayer of Remembrance
Merciful Father, hear our prayers
   for all those who died in the two World Wars
   and other violent conflicts since.
As we renew our faith in your Son,
   whom you raised from the dead,
   strengthen our hope that all our departed brothers and sisters
   will share in the peace and joy of everlasting life with you.
Amen.

Prayers this week

For those who have died; especially past pupils and teachers.

Assembly idea

1 The Gospel story of Zacchaeus is easily dramatised or presented as a part-reading.

2 Ask the form to mention anyone in their families who has died in the past twelve months. Then suggest a short silence (20-30 seconds) while these people are remembered, and any others who may be recalled. Follow with the *Prayer of Remembrance*.

Thirty-second Week
in Ordinary Time (C)

Remembrance Sunday

Theme	*God of the living and of the dead*

The whole human race forms one family. This was made clear when Jesus asked us to call God 'Daddy' (Abba) or 'Father'. This family, with God at its head, is absolutely vast, including not only those on planet earth at this moment but all those humans who have ever lived – to whom, of course, in some way or other, we are all related. Catholics call this the 'Communion of Saints' which explains why holy people of the past (saints) are asked to speak to God for us. We also pray for those who have died.

Reading of the week

Luke 20:27-38

Prayer of the week

Father of the human family,
   you created our planet and each of us
   to give you glory and praise.
May we support and help each other
   as we learn to love and praise you.
Amen.

Quotation of the week

The final heartbeat for the Christian is not the mysterious conclusion to a meaningless existence. It is, rather, the grand beginning to a life that will never end. (James Dobson)

Alternative reading

2 Maccabees 7:1-2, 9-14

• 16th November

St Edmund Rich, Archbishop of Canterbury
A learned and saintly bishop who was best remembered as a teacher; he experienced visions to do with the Holy Trinity (hence his symbol of three suns). He died in 1240.

Prayer of the day

Father of all wisdom and knowledge,
   your holy bishop, Edmund,
   was devoted to teaching
   and helping others to learn about you.
May we grow daily in our knowledge and love of you.
Amen.

Prayers this week

For those who, at this time, are grieving the death of a loved one.

Assembly idea

Give out a slip of paper to each of the form. Ask one third of the group to write down the name of a saint; ask each of the second third to write the name of someone they know and love; and ask the third section to write down the name of someone from their family who has died.

   Read out the introduction on this page (or an adaptation of it). In turn, as many as there is time for, read out a name from each group: a saint, a loved one, a deceased family member. Close with the *Prayer of the week*.

Thirty-third Week
of Ordinary Time (C)

Theme

Hard work

It is not only our teachers – and when we get a job, our employers – who expect us to work hard: God does too! Being idle and lazy is condemned in the Bible. Paul says to the Christians of Thessalonica, 'We order you to go on quietly working.' Idleness is a sin because it is unfair, making life more difficult for others and being unprepared to do our share. God expects us to work, and so help to improve the quality of life for everyone.

Reading of the week   2 Thessalonians 3:7-12

Prayer of the week   Father, Creator of the universe,
    you made everything out of nothing.
Help us in our daily work,
    to do our best and develop into the caring people
    that you want us to be.
Amen

Quotation of the week   Idleness is the enemy of the soul. (St Benedict)

Alternative reading   1 Thessalonians 5:12-15

• 22nd November   *St Cecilia, Patroness of Musicians*
A Christian woman, who in third-century Rome converted her husband to her faith and shortly afterwards was imprisoned and executed for the same faith. One of the most famous of the Roman women martyrs, no one today knows how she came to be chosen as the patron of musicians.

Prayer of the day   Lord of mercy,
    be close to those who call upon you.
With St Cecilia to help us,
    hear and answer our prayers.
Amen.

Prayer this week   For those in our country who cannot find work and are disheartened and feel rejected.

Assembly idea   Put the following words on the board: 'No pain, no gain; no guts, no glory'. Explain that when Sarah Hardcastle (who won an Olympic silver medal and several bronzes for swimming) turned up for training at 5 o'clock each morning, she changed in front of these words which she had put up to remind her of the cost involved. It worked!

Thirty-fourth Week
in Ordinary Time (C)

National Youth Sunday

Theme   *Christ the King*

The last Sunday of the Church's year (we start a new year next week) is celebrated with a day dedicated to Christ the Universal King. It is to remind us of the Christian belief that the victorious and triumphant risen Christ will come again in glory at the end of the world. On this day we celebrate 'Youth', our hope for our future.

Reading of the week   Luke 23:35-43

Prayer of the week   Father, all-powerful God of love,
    you raised Jesus from death to life
    and he is now with you, in glory,
    as King of Creation.
May all the world rejoice in his peace,
    glory in his justice, to live in his love. Amen.

Quotation of the week   Power in complete subordination to love – that's a definition of the kingdom of God. (William Temple)

• National Youth Sunday   Young people are the hope of the future of the People of God, so the year ends with thoughts and prayers for all young people, their youth groups and associations, and all those who work with young people.

Alternative readings   John 18:33-37
Matthew 25:31-46

• 30th November   *St Andrew, Apostle and Patron of Scotland*
Andrew, like his brother, Simon Peter, was a fisherman who was called by Jesus to be one of his twelve Apostles. He is believed to have died a martyr's death at Patras in Achaia. He is patron of Greece and Russia as well as Scotland.

Prayer of the day   Lord, in your kindness
    hear our prayers.
You called Andrew to preach the Gospel
    and witness to its truth.
May we share the same deep faith
    and grow in your love. Amen.

Prayers this week   For all Christian young people, that they may remain true and faithful to their commitment to Christ.

Assembly idea   *Christ the King*
Invite the local Youth chaplain or Diocesan/Deanery youth worker to speak briefly on the needs of youth, or why this Sunday is linked with young people. (See Year A, page 22, and B, page 64, for other ideas.)

First Week
of Advent (A)

Theme

Advent – Be prepared

This is 'Happy New Year' week, because Sunday saw the beginning of a new year in the Christian calendar. 'Advent' – the 'Coming Season' – has begun and all Christians are asked to 'Be prepared' and 'Stay awake' to the real meaning of Christmas. This is the season of preparation, for the coming of Christ as a babe, as the Good News and as judge at the end of time.

Reading of the week

Matthew 24:37-44

Prayer of the week

Father in heaven,
   our hearts desire the warmth of your love.
Increase our longing for Christ our Saviour
   and give us the strength to grow in love
   as we wait for his coming.
Amen.

Quotation of the week

Time is full of eternity. As we use it so shall we be. (Henry Manning)

Alternative readings

Romans 13:11-14
Jeremiah 33:14-16

• 8th December

The Immaculate Conception of the Blessed Virgin Mary
This day celebrates the 'specialness' of Mary, from the moment of her conception (this is not the same as the Virgin Birth). She was chosen, even before her own birth, for the wonderful privilege of being the mother of Jesus, the Son of God. It is summed up in the words 'Hail Mary, full of grace'.

Prayer of the day

Father, you prepared the Virgin Mary,
   even from the first moment of her conception
   to be the worthy mother of your Son.
Help us, by her prayers,
   to live in your presence without sin.
Amen.

Prayers this week

For people who do not know and understand the true meaning of Christmas.

Assembly idea

Acquire (a form member or a member of staff may be able to help) an article of Scout/Guide uniform – for example, a belt, beret or hat badge – with the motto 'Be prepared' on it. Show the item and speak briefly about the philosophy behind Baden Powell units (service). 'Be prepared': for what? Answer: to help others. A good motto for Advent.

Second Week of Advent (A)

Bible Sunday

Theme

Change your ways

If you are going out for the evening, you wash and change your clothes. John, son of Zechariah and nicknamed 'the Baptist', told the people that they had to be baptised (wash) and change their lives if they were going to be ready to welcome the Messiah. That is what Advent is about: preparing ourselves for the coming of the Messiah which we celebrate at Christmas. Let us all improve our behaviour to family and friends.

Reading of the week

Matthew 3:1-12

Prayer of the week

Father, in heaven,
   your Son's birthday draws near.
May the greed and selfishness
   which tempt so many people at this time of the year,
   not blind us to the real meaning of his coming.
Amen.

Quotation of the week

To bend a crooked stick straight, we bend it the contrary way. (Michel de Montaigne)

Alternative readings

Isaiah 11:1-10
Mark 1:1-8

• 14th December

St John of the Cross, Doctor of the Church
A great sixteenth-century Carmelite priest who suffered many difficulties in helping to reform the Spanish Church. Famous for his books on prayer; classics which are still studied and found inspiring today.

Prayer of the day

Father, you gave St John of the Cross
   the courage to be constantly unselfish.
May we follow his example
   and learn to put others first.
And so come finally into your everlasting love.
Amen.

Prayers this week

For children who are orphans and have no family of their own. May they find happiness this Christmas.

Assembly idea

Ask, 'How does your father/mother change a light bulb?' Very often they reach up, twist the bulb, remove it and put in a new one. We need to do the same in our lives. We need to reach up to God, turn ourselves round – so that we behave better – and then shine for others.

Third Week of Advent (A)

Theme

Rejoice! The Lord is coming

We all want one thing – to be happy. That's how it should be, because God made us for happiness. Television, magazines, the National Lottery – all suggest that happiness comes from having more and more, being famous and successful, and so on. The baby of Bethlehem had none of those things. Later in life he taught the secret of happiness: it comes and stays with us if we lovingly do things for others, if we are unselfish.

Reading of the week

Matthew 11:2-11

Prayer of the week

Father, the whole world looks with eagerness
   to the celebration of the birthday of Jesus.
May we, in our lives,
   know the real meaning of happiness
   and find it in the peace
   that your Son promises to all who follow him.
Amen.

Quotation of the week

Those who bring sunshine to the lives of others cannot keep it from themselves. (James M. Barrie)

Alternative reading

James 5:7-10

Prayers this week

For all children around the world, especially those whose parents are too poor to make Christmas special.

Assembly idea

As cards and gifts are being exchanged this week, ask the form to remember the pupils who are not their friends, especially any who find it difficult to make friends. Great happiness can be given to others by a surprise card or gift, or a genuine smile and a helping hand.

Second Week
after Christmas (A)

Theme	*Human Dignity*

I know I'm special; we each believe that we are special. We have this sense of uniqueness. We have just celebrated the reason for this: Christmas celebrates the amazing belief that God became one of us. God lived among us as a human being! From that belief it follows that the whole of human life has been penetrated by the Divine; human beings have a dignity because 'the Word was made flesh' and 'lived among us'.

Reading of the week

John 1:1-18

Prayer of the week

Father of our Lord Jesus Christ,
   the simple dignity of the baby of Bethlehem
   reminds us of our own dignity
   as your adopted children.
May we find your love in each other
   and reflect it in our lives.
Amen.

Quotation of the week

Scrubbing floors and emptying bedpans has as much dignity as the Presidency. (Richard M. Nixon)

Alternative reading

Ephesians 1:3-6

• The Epiphany

(When the Feast of Epiphany falls on a Saturday or Monday, it is celebrated on the Sunday. If this occurs the school may like to celebrate the Epiphany on the Monday.) This is the 'Showing Day' because the word 'Epiphany' means 'showing'; the child Jesus is shown to the astrologers from the East. These non-Jews (Gentiles) represent all those who, over the centuries, from all the nations of the earth, would follow Christ.

Prayer of the day

Father of Light,
   today we celebrate how your Son, Jesus,
   the Light of the World,
   was revealed to people of faith.
Make our faith strong, that Christ
   may be revealed to us,
   in our daily life and contacts.
Amen.

Prayers this week

For the millions of young teenage girls who are slaves in Asian countries, like Thailand.

Assembly idea

Acquire (RE department may be able to help) five or six candles of different size, shape and colour, and display them. Ask the form, 'If these were people which one would be the most important?' (The tall one, the red one, etc.?) Listen to replies, then, without comment, light each candle. (Answer: they are all of equal value. Just as one flame lights them all and all give an equal light so the same life and spirit of God lives in each person.)

Second Week in Ordinary Time (A)

Theme

The Servant Messiah

Jesus was a man for others. Although he could command respect, simply because he was the Messiah, he did not; he lived humbly, attending to the needs of others, like a servant. He was always at people's beck and call. One of the most enduring pictures of Jesus and his service of others was when he washed his friends' feet at the Last Supper. He directed that we should provide the same kind of humble service.

Reading of the week
Isaiah 49:3, 5-6

Prayer of the week
Almighty and ever-present Father,
    you see all that we do,
    but your glance is a look of love.
May you see us imitating your Son, Jesus Christ,
    who was not proud and full of his own importance,
    but humbly helped everyone as a servant.
Amen.

Quotation of the week
The service that counts is the service that costs. (Howard Hendricks)

Alternative readings
John 13:1-16
Philippians 2:5-11

• 18th-25th January
Week of Prayer for Christian Unity
The followers of Christ are divided. The Christian Family (that is all those who have been baptised in whatever denomination) consists of 1.8 billion people worldwide, split into three parts: Catholics, Orthodox and Protestants. Jesus wanted his family to remain united, and this week we pray that his wish will be fulfilled.

Prayer for Unity Week
Father of all, your Son prayed
    that all his followers would remain united.
Sadly, over the centuries, we have become separated;
    brothers and sisters of the same family,
    but not united.
We pray, this week, that all Christians
    will love and respect one another
    and work hard to become
    one united family once again.
Amen.

Prayers this week
For all the Christians of our local churches, whatever their denomination.

Assembly ideas
1 Acquire the Week of Prayer leaflet available from Churches Together in England and Wales. Follow the daily intention and use the thought and prayer provided.

2 Ring up a local minister and invite him/her in to take an assembly.

Third Week
in Ordinary Time (A)

Theme

Christ, our Light

Being frightened of the dark is something we associate with young children, but there are a surprising number of older people who have retained the fear. Without the message and example of Jesus, life can be like stumbling around in the dark – and with all the fears that go with that. The big questions of life – 'What is life for?', 'Is death the end?' – leave some people in the dark. We have Christ's answers: he is the Light of the World.

Reading of the week

Matthew 4:12-23

Prayer of the week

Almighty and ever-present Father,
   your loving eye is always on us,
    and even the tensions and frustrations of life
    cannot destroy your plans for us.
Help us to believe in you and trust you,
   no matter what happens.
Amen.

Quotation of the week

From a little spark may burst a mighty flame. (Dante Alighieri)

Alternative reading

Isaiah 8:23-9:3

• 25th January

The Conversion of St Paul
Today marks the end of the Week of Prayer for Christian Unity. Saul was the Jewish Pharisee who was converted very dramatically on the road to Damascus. (His name was changed to Paul to mark that.) He proved to be not only a great missionary of the Good News, but also a great and vital thinker who helped to shape and develop the Christian message.

Prayer of the day

God our Father,
   the Good News of Jesus
   was spread by Paul, your apostle.
Today we celebrate his conversion to the faith;
   may we remain true and faithful
   to the Christian Faith that he preached.
Amen.

Prayers this week

For all those young people who were baptised as Christians but have given up following Christ.

Assembly idea

If the school has an Easter candle, borrow it to light in the form room. (If not, any large candle will do; the RE department may be able to help.) Talk about the symbolism of the Easter candle representing Christ, the Light of the World.

Fourth Week
in Ordinary Time (A)

Theme

Poor in spirit

Many children in the past grew up reading *Mister Men* books; one favourite was *Mister Topsy Turvy* who lived an upside-down life. Jesus asks his followers to live by upside-down principles. What our world, our society, tells us is of value, Jesus contradicts. 'Happiness comes from having more and more' is what we hear; but Jesus says, 'Happy are the poor in spirit.' People tell us, 'Assert yourself, get to the top at any cost'; but Jesus says, 'Happy are the gentle.'

Reading of the week

Matthew 5:1-12

Prayer of the week

Father in heaven,
 from the days of Abraham and Moses
 you have gathered and formed a people,
 from whom you have expected love and obedience.
May our love and our willingness to do your will
 grow and develop.
We ask this through Christ, our Lord,
 who gave you complete obedience. Amen.

Quotation of the week

The person who is poor in spirit is the person who has realised that things mean nothing, and God means everything. (William Barclay)

Alternative readings

1 Corinthians 1:26-31
Zephaniah 2:3; 3:12-13

• 2nd February

The Presentation of the Lord (traditionally known as 'Candlemas')
On this day candles are blessed and held by the people during the reading of the Gospel, and then taken home. As the first-born son, Jesus was taken to the Temple to be presented to God. Mary and Joseph had to make an offering of two doves to 'buy' him back. This day celebrates that event.

Prayer of the day

All-powerful Father,
 Christ your Son was presented
 to you in the Temple.
May we offer ourselves to you each day,
 so that all we do may give you praise. Amen.

Prayers this week

For people who are so attached to having lots of money and possessions that they never take notice of God or the poor.

Assembly idea

Ask pupils (the day before) to bring in a treasured object, perhaps of sentimental value (all due security allowing for this). Ask how attached they are to these objects. If someone we loved asked us to throw it away, could we do that? No one is likely to, but God asks each of us always to put people first.

Fifth Week
in Ordinary Time (A)

Theme
          The light of example

We learn by example: we see and hear how our parents do things and we learn. Example is one of the most powerful forces on our planet. Christ's example of obedience to his Father, his courage in facing suffering, his willingness to forgive; the example of his whole life is very powerful. Christ expects his friends to give good example too: 'You are the light of the world,' he says.

Reading of the week
    Matthew 5:13-16

Prayer of the week
    Father, watch over us,
        for we are your family.
    Keep us safe from harm.
    May no action or thought of ours hurt others;
        for you love each of them, as you love us.
    Amen.

Quotation of the week
    Example is not the main thing in influencing others – it is the only thing. (Albert Schweitzer)

Alternative readings
    Isaiah 58:6-10
    1 Corinthians 2:1-5

Prayers this week
    For all teachers, everywhere, that they may teach not only by their words but by the example of their lives.

Assembly idea
    Bring in a powerful torch or spotlight and flash it around the room – if possible highlighting a feature not usually seen clearly. Jesus 'shone out', setting an example of how we should live. Jesus asks each of us to be a 'light in the world'.

Sixth Week
in Ordinary Time (A)

Theme

The Wisdom of God

The internet, e-mail, and all that we understand by information technology, has made access to information so easy. But with so much information and knowledge at our fingertips are we really better persons? Have we suddenly become *wise* as distinct from knowledgeable? Christ tells us that a simple uneducated person who lives faithfully by God's commandments can be wiser than the most educated of people.

Reading of the week

1 Corinthians 2:6-10

Prayer of the week

Father in heaven,
   the loving plan of your wisdom
   took flesh in Jesus Christ,
   and changed humankind's history
   by his command of perfect love.
May we be inspired by the same wisdom
   to seek and do your will.
Amen.

Quotation of the week

Common sense in an uncommon degree is what the world calls wisdom. (Samuel Taylor Coleridge)

Alternative reading

Ecclesiasticus 15:15-20

Prayers this week

For boys and girls around the world who have no access to an education.

Assembly idea

On a slip of paper write, 'Wisest person in the world', and on another write, 'Most knowledgeable person in the world'. Ask for two volunteers and give a slip to each. They tell the form who they are, and the form then decides which is the best person to be. Have another volunteer read 1 Corinthians 13:1-3 (or the *Reading of the week*) and ask if this is relevant to the discussion. Conclude with the *Prayer of the week*.

First Week of Lent (A)

Theme

Temptation

Everyone, even the Pope, is tempted. It is as much part of being a human as eating and sleeping. Temptation can make us stronger and better people *if* we learn how to resist it. Just as PE develops our bodies and the physical side to us, so temptation, if we can recognise what it is and resist it, develops the spiritual side of our personality.

Reading of the week

Matthew 4:1-11

Prayer of the week

Father, your Son resisted the temptations
　　of the devil, while fasting for forty days.
May we too resist temptation more strongly
　　during the forty days of Lent.
Assist us with your grace and strength.
Amen.

Quotation of the week

You are not tempted because you are evil; you are tempted because you are human (Fulton J. Sheen)

Alternative readings

Genesis 2:15-17, 3:1-7
Luke 4:1-13

Prayers this week

For all the people in the world who are hungry, not through choice but because they are so poor they cannot help themselves.

• The meaning of Lent

Lent prepares us for Easter, as Advent prepares us for Christmas. Easter is the most important of the Christian festivals. Christians think of themselves as the 'Easter People' and believe that Jesus not only rose from the dead but is still with his followers. So Lent is to be taken seriously because it helps us to celebrate Easter well and to appreciate the real meaning of the death and resurrection of Jesus.

• Ways to make Lent special

1　It is a time for a *change of heart* – a time for a fresh and closer look at ourselves and the way we live our lives. What needs to be done? We *can* change for the better; we must try.

2　It is a time for *concern for others* – a time for caring. Being concerned about others is a powerful weapon in our fight against our selfishness. We *can* do more and be more generous; we must try.

3　It is a time for *prayer that costs* – a time to make a real effort to speak regularly to our best friend, to Christ our Lord. We *can*, in our own private time, make an effort to pray; we must try.

Second Week of Lent (A)

Theme

The Glory of God

God's glory is hidden most of the time; we only get glimpses of it from time to time – for example, in the beauty of a sunset or in the smile of a young child, or in the unexpected kindness of a stranger. A short time before Jesus' death, God allowed the glory of his Son to be seen by his friends, the Apostles, Peter, James and John. This was to remind them that, although it was hidden, God's glory is real and always there.

Reading of the week

Matthew 17:1-9

Prayer of the week

Father of Light,
    pour the light of your love into our minds and hearts,
    that we may live good lives and give you the glory
    for the good things we achieve.
Amen.

Quotation of the week

We are his glory, when we follow his ways. (Florence Nightingale)

Alternative readings

John 15:5-8
2 Timothy 4:1-8

• Giving up for Lent

It is well known that Catholics 'give something up' for Lent. If this means giving up a bad habit, that must be good. If it means giving up, for example, eating sweets, that could be good news for your teeth! Unless, of course, 'giving up' makes you bad-tempered and difficult to get on with. Kindness and love must never suffer when we make a sacrifice to fight our selfishness. It might be better to 'take up' something: for example, going to Mass regularly throughout Lent; or saying night prayers better each evening; or making a special effort, every day of Lent, to help at home.

Prayers this week

For people in the music industry, that they may give glory to God for their talents.

Assembly idea

Start an assembly by reading *Giving up for Lent*. Follow with a brainstorm of ideas of what might be done for Lent. Ask for a minute of silence during which each person has the opportunity to decide what to do, and, if they wish, make a promise to God to do their best to keep the resolution. End with the *Prayer of the week*.

Third Week
of Lent (A)

Theme

The dignity of women

Feminists alert us to any inequality which arises between the sexes. Jesus lived at a time when women were treated badly as second-class members of the community. He was revolutionary in the way he treated women; he gave them respect and numbered them among his closest friends. It was the women who were faithful to him at the foot of the cross, and they who had the honour of finding the empty tomb on Easter day.

Reading of the week John 4:5-42

Prayer of the week
Father of all goodness,
    our selfishness stands in the way
    of the generous love that we should show
    to our families and friends.
May we use this time of Lent
    to improve our lives.
Amen.

Alternative reading John 8:1-11

Prayers this week For women of the developing countries who are denied basic human rights and are often treated as slaves.

Assembly idea

1 *Review time* Half-way through Lent, how have each of us made Lent special and different so far? Ask the group: Have you kept your resolutions for Lent? (If you didn't make any it is not too late.) Have you prayed more? Done anything extra for others, especially people that you don't get on with?

2 Write the name 'Mary' on the board and ask how many women in the Gospel story are called by this name. There are at least four (Mother of Jesus, Mary Magdalene, Mary the sister of Lazarus, Mary the mother of James). In other words, it was a popular name at the time. Make a comment that the dignity of women, over the centuries, despite the social history, has been kept alive through this name and the honour given to Mary the Mother of Jesus.

Fourth Week of Lent (A)

Theme

Spiritual blindness

Many people are so involved in daily work, shopping, earning and spending money, that they do not seem aware of their own spiritual life and its needs. They feel an 'emptiness' inside which they try to satisfy by buying new and better things; but it never goes away. They do not realise that the 'space' inside can only be filled by knowing and loving God. They are spiritually blind and need Christ the Light.

Reading of the week   John 9:1-41

Prayer of the week

God our Father and Mother,
   you cared so much for us
   that you gave us your Son,
   as the Light of the World.
May we not be blind, but see the way that leads
   to a peaceful conscience and a good life.
Amen.

Alternative reading   Ephesians 5:8-14

Quotation of the week   To see one's darkness proves the presence of a great light. (Raoul Pius)

• 18th March   *St Patrick, Apostle of Ireland*
It was Patrick, the patron saint of Ireland, who took the Christian faith to Ireland, and established it there by his own courage and holiness of life.

Prayer of the day

God our Father,
   you sent St Patrick as a missionary to Ireland;
   may we too be your missionaries,
   showing everyone, by our lives,
   that you are a God of goodness and love.
Amen.

• 19th March   *St Joseph, Husband of Mary*
Joseph was the husband of Mary and the foster-father of Jesus. He was a village carpenter by trade. He is now the patron of the Catholic Church.

Prayer of the day

Almighty Father,
   you entrusted your Son into the care of St Joseph.
May his prayers help us to be caring
   and worthy of trust.
Amen.

Prayers this week   For young and old who have become marginalised in our society: the homeless, young people who can find no employment, victims of abuse, etc.

Fifth Week
of Lent (A)

Theme

Life after death

At this time of the year gardeners are preparing their gardens for the springtime sowing. Dried-up, dead-looking seeds are put into the prepared ground; within a few weeks a row of fresh green shoots has appeared – new life, the wonder of spring. Jesus died, was buried, but he rose up to new life. That is the central theme – and wonder – of Christianity. We too must die to selfishness and rise up to a new life of loving others.

Reading of the week

John 11:1-45

Prayer of the week

Father in heaven,
    the love of your Son led him to accept
    the suffering of the cross.
Change our selfishness into self-giving.
Help us to transform the darkness of this world's pain
    into the life and joy of Easter.
Amen.

Quotation of the week

Death is but a sharp corner near the beginning of life's procession down eternity. (John Ayscough)

Alternative readings

1 Corinthians 15:35-44
Hebrews 5:7-9

• 25th March

The Annunciation of the Lord
Mary, the young girl of Nazareth, is asked to be the mother of the Christ; she accepts. This event is nine months from Christmas Day and is the origin of Mother's Day, being the day on which Mary conceived by the special power of God.

Prayer of the day

God our Father,
    your Son became man and was born of the Virgin Mary.
May we remember and thank God for our own mothers
    at this time of the year.
Amen.

Prayers this week

For our parents, especially our mothers, who have done, and are doing, so much for us. We pray for their good health and happiness.

Assembly idea

Acquire a packet of seeds (beetroot are particularly suitable) but keep secret what the seeds will become. Go round the group placing one seed in each open palm. Ask if anyone can guess what the dried-up, dead-looking seed will become. After telling them, speak of the symbolism of Easter. A live chick comes out of what appears to be a stone; so Christ comes alive out of the dead tomb (hence Easter eggs).

Second Week of Easter (A)

Theme

Believing without seeing

Sometimes people say, 'I won't believe unless I see it.' One of the friends of Jesus, Thomas (nicknamed 'Doubting'), said it, when he heard that Jesus had been seen alive after his death. Jesus appeared again and said to Thomas, 'Come on, then, touch and see.' Thomas believed. One billion 800 million friends of Jesus today (Christians in the world) believe in the Risen Jesus without seeing. 'Happy are those who have not seen, but believe,' said Jesus.

Reading of the week

John 20:19-31

Prayer of the week

Heavenly Father and God of mercy,
    we do not look for Jesus among the dead,
    for he is alive.
Increase our faith that we may believe
    without looking for evidence.
May our faith and trust grow every day.
Amen.

Quotation of the week

For what is faith unless it is to believe what you do not see. (St Augustine)

Alternative readings

Mark 16:15-20
1 Peter 1:3-9

• 25th April

St Mark, Gospel writer
If John Mark, the secretary of St Peter, had not thought of writing down the Good News of Jesus, as preached by Peter, there would have been no Gospel of St Mark. It was the first to be written and became the model for the other three. (See the story of the mysterious young man in Mark 14:51-52.)

Prayer of the day

Almighty Father,
    you gave St Mark
    the privilege of proclaiming your Gospel.
May we profit by his wisdom
    and follow Christ more faithfully.
Amen.

Prayers this week

For all those adults who were received into the Church as new Catholics at Easter.

Assembly idea

The dramatic story of 'Doubting' Thomas could be acted out in the form room; or there could be a part-reading.

Third Week
of Easter (A)

Theme

Meeting Christ in the Eucharist

'I will be with you always,' Jesus promised his followers. 'Do this in memory of me,' Jesus said at the Last Supper. By breaking bread together and sharing the cup (in other words, by receiving Holy Communion), we are doing what he asked and we are making him present to us. We really meet with the Risen Christ in the sacrifice and the sacrament of the Eucharist.

Reading of the week

Luke 24:13-35

Prayer of the week

God our Father,
    may we look forward with hope
    to our own resurrection,
    for it is promised every time
    that we receive your Son in Holy Communion.
Amen.

Quotation of the week

The sheer stupendous quantity of the love of God which this ever-repeated action has drawn from obscure Christian multitudes through the centuries is in itself an overwhelming thought. (Gregory Dix)

Alternative reading

1 Corinthians 11:23-29

• 23rd April

St George, Protector of England
Many legends surround St George; all we know for sure is that he was a martyr who died for his faith in Christ, about 350. He was admired by the Crusaders from Europe who brought veneration of him back from the Holy Land.

Prayer of the day

Lord, hear the prayers of those
    who praise your mighty power.
As St George was ready to follow Christ
    in suffering and death,
    so may he be ready to help us in our weakness.
Amen.

Prayers this week

For the boys and girls in our local primary schools who are preparing to make their First Holy Communion in a few weeks' time.

Assembly idea

Write the word 'McDonalds' very large on the board. Ask why people go there. (To meet their friends and to eat.) We go to the Eucharist for the same reasons; to meet Jesus our friend and to eat. Just as we need to eat to keep our physical bodies alive, so we need to eat the spiritual food, the Body of Christ, to remain spiritually alive and well.

Fourth Week
of Easter (A)

**Week of Prayer
for Vocations**

Theme

The Good Shepherd

We don't see shepherds at work and have very fanciful ideas about them and their cuddly sheep. A real shepherd was a tough, outdoor man, who led mixed herds of sheep and goats which wandered stupidly all over the place. Jesus said that he was like a good shepherd who cares for us, his mixed herd. At times we wander rather senselessly all over the place. Following our Good Shepherd can give real meaning and direction to our lives.

Reading of the week   John 10:1-10

Prayer of the week
Almighty and ever-living God,
    please give us the strength and the courage
      that we need to follow Christ, our Good Shepherd.
May we trust him completely
    especially when life is confusing and hard.
Amen.

Quotation of the week   The more we depend upon God the more dependable we find he is. (Cliff Richard)

Alternative reading   Isaiah 40:9-11

• 1st May   *St Joseph, Foster-father of Jesus, Patron of all workers*
Joseph was entrusted by God with caring for and bringing up his Son; it was one of the most important roles ever fulfilled by anyone in history. The Church has entrusted all workers (most people) into the care of St Joseph, who knew what it was like to face a hard day of manual work.

Prayer of the day
God our Father, creator of the Universe,
    in every age of history you call people
      to develop their gifts and talents for the good of others.
With St Joseph as our model and guide,
    help us to find satisfying work and use it
    to benefit others as well as ourselves.
Amen.

• 3rd May   *St Philip and St James*
Little is known of these friends of Jesus, except that they accepted his invitation to follow him. They died heroic deaths for the Gospel and their love of Christ.

Prayers this week   For more and more generous people to help in our parishes, that Christ's love and care may reach more of those in need.

Fifth Week
of Easter (A)

Theme

Christ – the Way, the Truth and the Life

At the beginning of Christianity, before they were nicknamed 'Christians', the followers of Jesus called themselves 'The People of the Way'. Jesus had said, 'I am the Way, the Truth and the Life', and his followers realised that *the way* to a happy, fulfilled life was to follow the Way of the love of God and of other people. Jesus is *the* Way to God.

Reading of the week

John 14:1-12

Prayer of the week

God our Father,
   look upon us with love.
Your Son has showed us the way to live and to love.
He has given us the truth that will set us free
    to live lovingly as we follow
    such a wonderful friend and guide.
Amen.

Quotation of the week

Let us rejoice in the truth, wherever we find its lamp burning.
(Albert Schweitzer)

Alternative readings

John 6:35-40
1 John 3:18-24

Prayers this week

For Christians who are suffering for their faith today. In countries like the Sudan many Christians are persecuted for following Christ, the Way.

Assembly idea

Ask the group if they have ever been lost in an unfamiliar town. It's helpful if someone gives directions; however, it is so much better if a person actually takes you to the place you are looking for. Jesus does both; he tells us how to find our way in life (for example, 'Love one another'), and he is prepared to show us the way if we keep close to him through regular prayer.

Sixth Week
of Easter (A)

Theme

The spirit of truth

When a friend is going away for a long time, or for good, they often give a 'going away' gift; something to remember them by. Jesus did that; he promised before he died that he would give his friends the gift of the 'Spirit of Truth', the Holy Spirit. Good friends of Jesus, who try hard to follow him, are transparently honest and sincere; they often do not realise how wonderfully they show that they possess the gift of the Spirit.

Reading of the week

John 14:15-21

Prayer of the week

Ever-living God,
   fill us with the Spirit of your truth, love and peace.
Help us to live by the truth
   and enjoy the peace that only you can give.
Amen.

Quotations of the week

The name of God is Truth. (Hindu proverb)

Every truth without exception – and whoever may utter it – is from the Holy Spirit. (St Thomas Aquinas)

Alternative readings

Acts 1:1-11
Luke 24:46-53

• Thursday

The Ascension of the Lord
The 'Going-up' or 'Ascension' of Christ brings to an end his appearances to his friends after the Resurrection. What happened on the first Ascension day is a little mysterious, but for believers it is the *promise* that matters: the promise that as Jesus lives now with his Father, so, after death, shall we; the promise that there *is* life after death.

Prayer of the day

Father in heaven,
   our thoughts turn to the reality
   of everlasting life with you,
   when we recall Christ's Ascension.
May we, one day, follow where he has led,
   and find our hope in his glory.
Amen.

Prayers this week

For people who are suffering from any form of mental illness or disorder.

Assembly idea

Start a game of *Chinese whispers*. A message (piece of news) is whispered to one pupil who must pass it on, with only the next person hearing it, around the whole room. The last person to receive the message repeats it aloud; the first then says what she/he was told. Comment on human communication; and, in contrast, how the Spirit has been passing on from century to century the truth about God and it is still the same today as it was when first spoken.

Seventh Week
of Easter (A)

World Communications Week

Theme

Listening to God

We are all much better at talking than listening. God must spend most of his time listening, because most of our prayer is 'asking'. It is a compliment to describe someone as 'a good listener', but we should all be good listeners. We should also be prepared to listen to God, by sitting quietly sometimes in silent prayer. God also speaks to us through other people – our friends, parents and teachers.

Reading of the week

John 17:1-11

Prayer of the week

Father, help us to respect others
    by being prepared to listen.
Patient listening is a sign of love.
May we show our love for you
    by being quiet sometimes
    and allowing you to speak to us.
Amen.

Quotation of the week

I have often regretted my speech, but never my silence. (Publilius Syrus)

Alternative reading

1 Peter 4:13-16

Prayers this week

Those who are handicapped by deafness; and those people who deliberately choose to be deaf to those in need.

Assembly idea

Make two lists on the board: first the good that comes from TV and radio programmes; and second the bad. Comment that we should select the good for ourselves and not support the evil. Follow with a prayer for those who make the programmes.

Prayer for those in the media

Almighty Father
    your Word of Truth lived among us
    and told us of you and your love.
May all those who work in the media
    tell us the truth, promote justice and peace
    and help us to live in harmony with one another.
Amen.

Pentecost
(Years A, B and C)

Theme

Come, Holy Spirit

Jesus promised to send a comforter, the Spirit of Love, to fill his followers with faith, courage and strength. He kept his promise, and the wonderful faith and courage of his followers spread the Church around the world. We 'see' that faith today in the courageous lives of Christians like Roy Castle, Chico Mendes, Oscar Romero and Mother Teresa (add or subtract names here). The 'spirit' that everyone admired in Roy (or whoever) was the Holy Spirit, the gift of God.

Reading of the week

John 20:19-23

Prayer of the week

Father of Light,
    from whom all good gifts come,
    send your Spirit into our lives,
    that we may be filled with the faith and courage
    which we need to live as faithful Christians
    in a troubled world.
Amen.

Quotation of the week

I pray thee, O God, that I may be beautiful within. (Socrates)

Alternative readings

Acts 2:1-11
1 Corinthians 12:3-7, 12-13

Prayers this week

For the Church, throughout the world, because Pentecost is the Birthday of the Church.

Assembly idea

Ask the form to sing *Happy Birthday*. They will ask whose birthday it is; tell them to put 'us' where the name would be and all will be revealed after singing it. Tell them that this week all Christians around the world are celebrating the birthday of the Church; and as Christians we are the Church.

Feast of
the Holy Trinity (A)

Theme

Glory to the Father, the Son and the Holy Spirit

On Sunday, around the world, all Christians celebrated the belief in the divine 'family' of the Godhead; three persons in one unity (Tri-unity) of being. This belief is unique to all Christians. It is impossible to imagine and very difficult to understand, but it is an essential belief for the Christian faith. The *Father*, who created everything, gave us the *Son* (or 'the *Word*') who rescued us and gave us his *Spirit*, the Spirit of faith, hope and love.

Reading of the week

John 3:16-18

Prayer of the week

Father, you sent us your Son
    to bring us the truth,
    and your Spirit to make us holy.
Through them we come to know
    the mystery of your life.
Help us to worship you,
    Father, Son and Holy Spirit.
Amen.

• 27th May

St Augustine, first Archbishop of Canterbury
Augustine was a reluctant missionary, accompanied by 40 other Benedictine monks, who, 1,400 years ago, landed near Ramsgate and set about converting the people of Kent to Christianity. He converted the King of Kent and became the first Archbishop of Canterbury.

• Thursday

The Body and Blood of Christ (The Feast of Corpus Christi)
Just as in our human life we need food and drink, so in our spiritual life we need Christ to nourish and sustain us. He feeds us with himself, with his words, through Scripture; and with the Sacrament of his Body and his Blood. As we eat together the sacred bread and wine, we share with one another, so the community is made strong as we grow personally in strength.

Prayer of the day

Lord Jesus Christ,
    we believe that you live among us
    and we worship your presence
    in the sacrament of your Body and Blood.
May the same Body and Blood give us strength
    to live the Christian life faithfully.
Amen

Prayers this week

For those who work for Christian unity so that soon all may share the same sacrament at the altar of Christ.

Ninth Week
in Ordinary Time (A)

Gospel: Matthew 7:21-27

Theme

Doing God's will

We all like to have our own way! Doing what we are told does not come easily. In Old Testament times God expected the Jews to keep the Law. Jesus said, 'A new commandment I give you . . . love one another.' Jesus said that if we follow his words we will be building on a rock; we will have a firm foundation to our lives if we do God's will.

Reading of the week Matthew 7:21-27

Prayer of the week
Father,
   your love never fails.
Hear our call.
Keep us from danger
   and provide for all our needs.
Amen.

Quotation of the week If God sends us on stony paths, he provides strong shoes.
(Corrie Ten Boom)

Alternative readings Deuteronomy 11:18, 26-28
Romans 3:21-25, 28

• Friday *The Sacred Heart of Jesus (Gospel: Matthew 11:25-30)*
Cards with hearts on are sent on Valentine's Day; we associate the human heart with love. The symbol of the heart of Jesus stands for that amazing love of Jesus that took him to the cross where his heart was pierced.

Prayer of the day
Father,
   we rejoice in all the gifts of love we have received,
   and especially for the wonderful love of Jesus,
   our Lord and Saviour.
Teach us to show that love
   by love-filled service to our brothers and sisters.
Amen.

Alternative readings 1 John 4:7-16
John 19:31-37

Prayers this week For those who are imprisoned for their faith or political beliefs; for the work of Amnesty International for prisoners of conscience.

Assembly idea Read aloud Deuteronomy 11:18, 26-28. Ask if anyone knows how Jewish men keep this command of God today. The RE department will be able to help with an illustration.

Theme

Showing mercy

Because God is good, all goodness, he is completely fair. He is a just God. But God is also loving and kind, and therefore he is full of mercy too. God has to balance justice with mercy. Christ asks us to try to do the same: we must act fairly but be prepared to punish people who are not just. *However*, we must also be merciful and not act in a vengeful way. Condemn the sin, but forgive the sinner.

Reading of the week

Matthew 9:9-13

Prayer of the week

God of wisdom and love,
   from you all goodness comes;
   help us, who have done wrong,
   to return to a life of thoughtfulness and love.
Amen.

Alternative readings

Hosea 6:3-6
Romans 9:14-18

• 13th June

St Anthony of Padua, Doctor of the Church
Anthony, who lived in the thirteenth century, had such a great love of God that he planned to sail to Africa and die a martyr trying to convert the Saracens. He was shipwrecked on the Italian coast, met St Francis and became a Franciscan friar and a world-famous preacher. (See also Year C, page 87)

Quotation from St Anthony
Consider every day special; have the same enthusiasm today as you had when you started something new.

Prayer of the day

Almighty God,
   you have given St Anthony to us
   as a ready helper in time of need.
With his assistance
   may we follow Christ more faithfully.
Amen.

Prayers this week

For those whose lives are miserable because they cannot forgive others and nurture resentment and hate.

Assembly idea

Develop the following outline story. A young boy was sent to the Headteacher for a misdemeanour. The Head said, 'You are usually a good boy, so this is what I'll do.' He reached for a notebook and a pencil. 'I will write your name, in pencil, in my notebook. If you do not come back within the next year, I will rub your name out. If you do I shall write it in ink and take further action.' Discuss.

Eleventh Week
in Ordinary Time (A)

Theme

Missionaries of Christ

It is a shocking fact that, on average, twelve men and women in the world die every year for being missionaries. That is, twelve Christians who have gone to a foreign country, like Indonesia, are killed for trying to teach the Good News of Jesus and live it in very difficult conditions for the love of Christ. Every year, since Jesus first sent them over 1,950 years ago, brave people have answered the call of Jesus to be missionaries.

Reading of the week

Matthew 9:36-10:8

Prayer of the week

Almighty Father,
   your Son asks us to be missionaries;
   he asks us to spread his Good News.
We can only do this with your help and strength,
   which we ask through Christ, our Lord.
Amen.

Quotation of the week

Your love has a broken wing if it cannot fly across the sea.
(Maltbie D. Babcock)

Alternative reading

Matthew 28:16-20

• 20th June

St Alban, the first British martyr
It was a case of mistaken identity, but Alban was happy to take the priest's place. Alban was arrested in Verulam (which became St Albans as a result of his death) in third-century Britain, for helping a priest to escape. He was Britain's first martyr.

Prayer of the day

Father, we celebrate the memory of Alban,
   the first Christian to die for you in our country.
Give us the strength to be faithful to you
   and the courage to admit that we are Christians.
Amen.

Prayers this week

For the priests and religious brothers and sisters who risk their lives, in developing countries, to spread the Good News of Jesus.

Assembly idea

Find the story of someone who has died in the last year for the Gospel (such stories will be found in *The Tablet, Far East,* etc.; the RE department may be able to help). Ask a member of the form to read it out; after suitable comment, follow with *Prayer of the week.*

Twelfth Week
in Ordinary Time (A)

Theme

Do not fear

The lives of many people are haunted by fear and anxiety – fear of ill health, of death, fear of failure and rejection, of not being loved. Repeatedly in the Bible the words 'Do not be afraid' and 'Do not fear' are found. If we have faith in God – that is, trust in him – we have no need to fear. If you love someone, you trust them. If we loved God more, we would trust him more and we would fear nothing.

Reading of the week Matthew 10:26-33

Prayer of the week Loving Father,
  you are the guide and protector of all your people,
   female and male, poor and rich.
  Whatever our situation or role in life,
   be always near, for we place all our trust in you.
  Amen.

Quotation of the week The only thing we have to fear is fear itself. (Franklin D. Roosevelt)

Alternative readings Jeremiah 20:10-13
  1 John 4:13-18

• 24th June *The Birthday of John the Baptist*
  Jesus described his cousin John as 'the greatest man born of woman'. John had a unique job to do; he prepared the way for a new age, the Christian Age. Today is John's birthday.

Prayer of the day All-powerful God,
  help us to walk where John the Baptist indicates;
  help us to follow your Son, Jesus Christ,
   and keep faithfully to his teaching.
  Amen.

Prayers this week For any members of our School community who live more in fear, even in their homes, than in love and peace.

Assembly idea Ask the form if they were afraid of the dark when they were small children. Ask if anyone is afraid of spiders! Read the words of Jesus in Matthew 10:29 (about sparrows), then ask the form to sit quietly and think of anything (or anyone) that is frightening them at the moment. Close with the *Prayer of the week*.

Thirteenth Week
in Ordinary Time (A)

Theme

Following Christ

Sometimes in our schools we come across pupils who want to have the reputation of being 'hard' or 'tough'. Well, you have to be hard or tough to be a friend and follower of Jesus. It calls for self-sacrifice, effort and courage, especially when people mock you. It's not easy to live by the standards of Christ; it's much easier to do what everyone else does – that's why the weak drop out. Happiness comes from doing the hard thing.

Reading of the week
Matthew 10:37-42

Prayer of the week
Father in heaven,
  you call us to reject the darkness of selfish pleasure-seeking,
  and walk in the light of Christ.
May we accept the offer of his friendship;
  and please give us the courage to live
  as true friends of Christ.
Amen.

Quotation of the week
True Christianity is love in action. (David O. Mckay)

Alternative readings
Luke 9:51-62
Galatians 5:1, 13-18

• 3rd July
St Thomas, Apostle and friend of Jesus
Thomas did us a great service by not, at first, believing that Jesus had risen. He doubted and we can doubt along with him; his experience can help us. (Read John 20:19-31.) Tradition has it that Thomas took the Gospel to India.

Prayer of the day
Almighty Father,
  as we honour the Apostle Thomas,
  may we feel the help of his prayers in our lives,
  as we try to follow Christ faithfully.
Amen.

Prayers this week
For all young people who have recently been confirmed in their parishes, that they may continue to follow Christ faithfully.

Assembly idea
Asks who supports *Manchester United* or *Liverpool* or *Arsenal* (or other teams as appropriate). A little rivalry may occur but do not let this build. Comment on what following a team means – wearing their colours, reading about the players, etc. The same goes for Jesus and his team, the *Twelve Apostles*. We must wear Jesus' colours and read about what he expects of us. There could be a short discussion about what colour is suggested by 'Love your neighbour'. Follow with the *Prayer of the week*.

Fourteenth Week
in Ordinary Time (A)

Theme

Gentleness

These days the word 'gentle' is more often associated with products for sale than people. 'Gentle on your skin' means being soft; but the word really means 'kind', 'courteous' or 'caring'. Jesus describes himself as gentle: 'Learn from me, for I am gentle . . .' We live in a hard and cynical world, a violent age; and we need gentle people, like the kind and caring Jesus, to show that there are other, better ways to live.

Reading of the week

Matthew 11:25-30

Prayer of the week

Father,
> through the gentle obedience of your Son
> you saved a hard and fallen world.
May that gentleness inspire us to learn from Christ,
> and be more gentle and caring in our daily lives.
Amen.

Quotation of the week

Nothing is so strong as gentleness, nothing so gentle as real strength. (St Francis of Sales)

Alternative readings

1 Peter 3:8-17
Ephesians 4:1-6

• 11th July

St Benedict, Patron of Europe
We hear so much about Europe and European union; most people forget that Europe was once united in the Catholic faith. St Benedict, who died in 547, did more for the unity of Europe than any other individual; through his hundreds of Benedictine monasteries throughout Europe he provided education and health care, which were great forces for the spread of culture and civilisation.

Prayer of the day

God our Father,
> you made St Benedict
> an outstanding educator and guide,
> unifying Europe in the Christian faith.
Grant that we may, like him, value education
> and all that advances the common good.
Amen.

Prayers this week

For our Catholic schools (many founded by the Benedictines), that they may be caring communities of culture and excellence.

Assembly idea

Write the proverb 'A gentle answer turns away wrath but a harsh word stirs up anger' (Proverbs 15:1) on the board. Use these questions for a brief discussion: Is it true in your experience? Do you mistake *gentleness* for *softness*? Is a teacher who acts gently thought to be soft? Follow up a few ideas, and close with the *Prayer of the week*.

Fifteenth Week
in Ordinary Time (A)

Theme

Respecting nature

On the Continent people usually go to the sea or the mountains for their holidays. In Britain many people chase off to find the sun. For a few weeks we are more in touch with nature than we usually are in our towns and cities. The sea, mountains and the warmth of the sun are all God's gifts to us, and we should appreciate them as such – and respect and look after the environment so that it will not be spoilt.

Reading of the week

Isaiah 55:10-11

Prayer of the week

God of Creation,
 we thank you for the beauty of our planet
 and for the joys of being out in the open air.
May we love and respect all that you have made
 and keep it unspoilt. Amen.

Alternative reading

Genesis 1:29-31
Genesis 2:7-9, 15

• 23rd July

St Bridget of Sweden
This Bridget was born in Sweden in 1303 and must be distinguished from the Irish St Bridget of the sixth century. As a wife and mother Bridget was happy, but became famous in later life, when as a widow she had many visions and founded a famous teaching order, the Bridgetines.

Prayer of the day

Lord our God,
 you revealed the secrets of heaven to St Bridget.
May we come to know and love you, as she did. Amen.

• 25th July

St James, Apostle
James was the brother of John, and one of Jesus' closest friends. He was present when Jesus cured Jairus' daughter and at the Transfiguration. He was beheaded by King Herod Agrippa in 42.

Quotation from St James
Every good and perfect gift is from above, coming down from the Father of light.

Prayer of the day

Almighty Father,
 by the martyrdom of St James
 you blessed the work of the early Church.
May his courage give us encouragement
 and his prayers give us strength
 to be faithful to our faith. Amen.

Prayers this week

For our environment, that it may be respected and cared for.

Prayers for Occasional Use

Traditional prayers

Act of faith
My God, I believe in you
and all that your Church teaches,
because you have said it,
and your word is true.

Act of hope
My God, I hope in you,
for grace and for glory,
because of your promises,
your mercy and power.

Act of charity
O my God, I love you with my whole heart
and above all things,
because you are infinitely good and perfect;
and I love my neighbour as myself
for love of you.
Grant that I may love you more and more in this life,
and in the next for all eternity.

Act of contrition
O my God, because you are so good,
I am very sorry that I have sinned against you,
and by the help of your grace
I will try not to sin again.

Prayer of dedication
Lord Jesus,
I give you my hands to do your work.
I give you my feet to go your way.
I give you my eyes to see as you do.
I give you my tongue to speak your words.
I give you my mind that you may think in me.
I give you my spirit that you may pray in me.
Above all,
I give you my heart that you may love in me,
your Father, and all humankind.
I give you my whole self that you may grow in me,
so that it is you, Lord Jesus,
who live and work and pray in me.

I confess   I confess to almighty God,
    to blessed Mary, ever virgin,
    to blessed Michael the archangel,
    to blessed John the Baptist,
    to the holy Apostles Peter and Paul,
    and to all the saints,
    that I have sinned exceedingly
    in thought, word and deed,
    through my fault, through my fault,
    through my most grievous fault.
Therefore I beseech the blessed Mary, ever virgin,
    blessed Michael the archangel,
    blessed John the Baptist,
    the holy Apostles Peter and Paul,
    and all the saints,
    to pray to the Lord our God for me.

Prayer of St Francis of Assisi   Lord, make me an instrument of your peace;
    where there is hatred let me sow love,
    where there is injury let me sow pardon,
    where there is doubt let me sow faith,
    where there is despair let me give hope,
    where there is darkness let me give light,
    where there is sadness let me give joy.
O Divine Master, grant that I may try
    not to be comforted but to comfort,
    not to be understood but to understand,
    not to be loved but to love.
Because it is in giving that we receive,
    it is in forgiving that we are forgiven,
    and it is in dying that we are born to eternal life.

Teach us, good Lord,
    to serve you as you deserve;
    to give and not to count the cost;
    to fight and not to heed the wounds;
    to toil, and not to seek for rest;
    to labour and to ask for no reward,
    save that of knowing that we do your will;
    through Jesus Christ our Lord.

God be in my head   God be in my head, and in my understanding;
God be in mine eyes, and in my looking;
God be in my mouth, and in my speaking;
God be in my heart, and in my thinking;
God be at mine end, and at my departing.
(Book of Hours)

137

For the faithful departed (The *De Profundis*)

Out of the depths I have cried to you, O Lord.
Lord, hear my voice.
Let your ears be attentive
    to the voice of my supplication.
If you, O Lord, shall observe iniquities,
    Lord, who shall endure it?
For with you there is merciful forgiveness;
    and by reason of your law
    I have waited for you, O Lord.
My soul has relied on his word;
    my soul has hoped in the Lord.
From the morning watch even until night
    let Israel hope in the Lord.
Because with the Lord there is mercy,
    and with him plentiful redemption.
And he shall redeem Israel from all his iniquities.
Eternal rest grant to them, O Lord.
And let perpetual light shine upon them.
May they rest in peace.
Amen.

O Lord, hear my prayer.
And let my cry come to you.

Let us pray:
O God, the Creator and Redeemer of all the faithful,
    grant to the souls of your servants departed
    the remission of all their sins,
    that through our pious supplications
    they may obtain that pardon which they have always desired;
    who lives and reigns for ever and ever.
Amen.

The memorare

Remember, O most loving Virgin Mary,
    that it is a thing unheard of,
    that anyone ever had recourse to your protection,
    implored your help, or sought your intercession,
    and was left forsaken.
Filled therefore with confidence in your goodness
    I fly to you, O Mother, Virgin of virgins.
To you I come,
    before you I stand,
    a sorrowful sinner.
Despise not my poor words,
O Mother of the Word of God,
    but graciously hear and grant my prayer.

138

Prayer of St Richard of Chichester

Thanks be to thee, my Lord Jesus Christ,
for all the benefits and blessings
which thou hast given to me,
for all the pains and insults
which thou hast borne for me,
O most merciful Friend, Brother and Redeemer.
May I know thee more clearly,
love thee more dearly,
and follow thee more nearly.

A modern version of this prayer

Day by day,
O dear Lord,
three things I pray:
to see thee more clearly,
love thee more dearly,
follow thee more nearly,
day by day
by day by day.

An Easter season prayer
I am risen

Reader   I am risen and am with you –
especially when you walk alone.

All   Lord, you are with us.
May we recognise you in our lives
and in the breaking of bread.

Reader   I am risen and am with you –
especially when you walk round in circles,
not knowing where to turn.

All   Lord, you are with us.
May we recognise you in our lives
and in the breaking of bread.

Reader   I am risen and am with you –
especially when you walk in darkness
and with desperation.

All   Lord, you are with us.
May we recognise you in our lives
and in the breaking of bread.

Reader   I am risen and am with you –
especially when you cannot walk,
when you stand still and feel 'all in'.

All   Lord, you are with us.
May we recognise you in our lives
and in the breaking of bread.

Reader   I am risen and am with you –
especially when you have come
to the end of your resources.

All   Lord, you are with us.
May we recognise you in our lives
and in the breaking of bread.

Final prayer   Christ is risen.
He doesn't stand there trembling,
     waiting for his disciples to defend him.
He wants to be announced, to be revealed.
People today are hungry for Christ
     and for the Good News he brings.
It is up to us to introduce Christ to them.
And so may the God of grace
     be helping your right hand,
          now and for ever, till your resurrection day.

Modern prayers

Showing our gratitude   O Lord, you have given us so much;
     life, in a world where many are never really well;
     food, in a world where many are hungry;
     education, in a world where many never have a chance;
     security, in a world where many are afraid.
We cannot pay you back,
     but show us what we can do for others;
     help us to remember children and young people in other lands,
     especially those who are hungry and diseased,
     those who are homeless and afraid,
     those who are unwanted and suffering.
Their words may be different from ours,
     but their hearts and minds are the same.
May we offer them the hand of friendship and love.

Offering friendship   Lord Jesus, you had friends
     and felt lonely and abandoned when,
     at the end of your life,
     they left you to suffer alone.
Help us to be good friends, loyal and reliable,
     ready to help whenever we can.
While we have special friends,
     please help us to be friendly with everyone,
     remembering that you asked us to love one another
     as you have loved us.
     Amen.

Living by the truth

O God, you can see my inmost thoughts
and know me better than I know myself.
You understand the impulses I feel,
the ambitions I have,
the silent loneliness I experience.
Forgive me my sins against truth –
the untruth within me, the half-truths,
the evasions, the exaggerations,
the trying silences that deceive,
the masks I wear before the world.
Help me to see myself as I really am,
and fill me with the courage I shall need
if I am to seek the truth and live in truth.

Coping with failure

Heavenly Father, things do not always go well.
We fail at home, with our friends, and here are school.
No one can be a success all the time.
Your Son, Jesus, knew what failure could be,
yet he did not give up.
Help us, too, to have faith and trust in you,
and believe that good can come from apparent failure.
Please use our failure to help us learn more about ourselves
and lead us to real personal growth.
We ask this through Jesus Christ, your Son.
Amen.

Understanding others

Almighty God,
help us not to judge others by appearances.
Help us, Lord, to understand that no matter
what race or colour we are, or what age,
we are all equally your sons and daughters.
May we never intentionally and deliberately
give hurt or offence to anyone.
Help us to realise that if we are all your sons and daughters,
that makes us brothers and sisters in your family.
We need your help to understand this
and live it out in our lives.
Amen.

Growing in maturity

Help me, Lord God,
not to take the easy way out
and repeat what I so often hear other people say:
'It's not my fault.'
May I have enough maturity
to accept responsibility for all my actions,
bad as well as good.
Amen.

Caring for God's creation

Heavenly Father, the Bible tells us
    that you are the creator of the world;
    that you made all the animals
    and brought them to the man, Adam, to name them.
You intended us to be in partnership with the animals,
    to watch over and care for them.
Stop, then, almighty God,
    and help us to stop,
    all the cruelty that we hear animals suffer.
There is no need for them to be hunted
    and trapped for their fur;
    no need for them to be experimented on for safer cosmetics;
    other ways can be found to make products safe.
We pray for our pets –
    may we respect and care for them.
We pray for guide dogs, guard dogs and other animals that work for
    human beings –
    may they be well loved and treated.
We pray for farm animals and poultry in factory farms –
    may they receive all they need for a happy life.
We pray for the wild animals of the countryside –
    may they suffer no cruelty from human beings.
We pray for all the animals caged in our zoos and parks –
    may their keepers provide them with enough space and care to ensure
    for them a dignified existence.
Father Creator, we pray for all animals,
    domestic and wild, that share our world –
    may none ever be abused or treated with cruelty,
    for we believe that you love all of your creation. Amen.

Postscript

Have you considered enlivening your assembly by using:

Music   could be used to illustrate a point or as a starting point. It is inadvisable to use the latest hit from a popular group – you can end up with adulation from one section of the form and ridicule from others who dislike that group. It's safer to stick with 'golden oldies'. For example:

Another day in paradise by Phil Collins is very appropriate for assemblies on the homeless, helping the poor, appreciation of what we have, serving others, etc.

From a distance by various artists including Bette Midler is useful for assemblies on peace, unity, ecology (our planet home), etc.

Story   is always popular – everyone enjoys a good story. Try to tell stories and not read them. It pays to learn a story so that you can tell it, because then there can be eye contact, movement and gestures which will bring the story to life; simple 'props' can also be used to effect. We are all full of stories; use events from your own life, and, of course, embroider them if necessary to make your point.

Posters   and pictures of all sorts can convey a message simply and very directly. Posters from CAFOD or Christian Aid, Amnesty International or even from McDonalds. (I asked my local McDonalds for a poster of a carton of Coca-cola and a Big Mac; in assembly I showed it and asked if Jesus would use coke instead of wine, if he celebrated the Last Supper today!)

Video   is *the* medium of today's youngsters so short extracts can be used, if there is a monitor and video recorder in the form room. Short scenarios from *EastEnders, Home and Away* and *Neighbours* have been used successfully.

Scripture   does not have to be read. For many years most Bible stories were told, long before they were written down. *Tell* the stories of Jesus as he and his friends did. Or use part readings or *The Dramatised Bible.*

Artefacts   and any object that can stimulate interest and reflection can be used. (I brought in a carpenter's tool that once belonged to my grandfather who had been a wheelwright. No one could guess what it was for; it was a spokeshave that was used to shape wooden spokes for a cart wheel. Jesus, as a carpenter, would have recognised it and most probably used one himself.)